# ELMER M. HAYGOOD

# They Came to Heal Us

## A Layman's Theory of Angelic Healing

iUniverse, Inc.
Bloomington

# They Came to Heal Us

*iUniverse books may be ordered through booksellers or by contacting:*

*iUniverse*
*1663 Liberty Drive*
*Bloomington, IN 47403*
*www.iuniverse.com*
*1-800-Authors (1-800-288-4677)*

*Because of the dynamic nature of the Internet, any web addresses or links contained in this book may have changed since publication and may no longer be valid. The views expressed in this work are solely those of the author and do not necessarily reflect the views of the publisher, and the publisher hereby disclaims any responsibility for them.*

*Any people depicted in stock imagery provided by Thinkstock are models, and such images are being used for illustrative purposes only.*

*Certain stock imagery © Thinkstock.*

*ISBN: 978-1-4620-2133-8 (sc)*
*ISBN: 978-1-4620-2134-5 (ebook)*

*Printed in the United States of America*

*iUniverse rev. date: 06/16/2011*

*What mean ye these stones? Joshua 4:6*

# Table of Contents

# List of Illustrations

# Introduction

> The first time we find angels mentioned in Scripture does not necessarily indicate their first arrival on the scene.
> (The Restored Church of God, www.thercg.org/articles/agms.html)

One of the most challenging areas of biblical studies is the definition and activities of angels. I believe that angels were more than messengers of God but had the ongoing responsibility for the physical preservation of mankind; they were the key to our survival. It is not conceivable that man could have continued to exist without their frequent intervention, because ancient events could have easily led to our extinction. According to historians, disasters, pestilence, and diseases were as numerous in prehistoric times as they are today, and prehistoric man was much less capable of dealing with them. Not only were there menacing natural threats, but man was subject to demonic infestations after his expulsion from the Garden of Eden. Man was then faced with the possibility of extinction from himself, especially since there was murder in the first family when Cain killed Abel.

Angels provided more assistance to ancient men than what is recorded in the Bible. I believe their involvement is memorialized in stone at megalithic sites throughout the world. I believe these sites are actually places of mass healings of people by angels in response to a great disaster in the ancient world of Pangaea:

> Before the advent of plate tectonics, however, some people already believed that the present-day continents were the fragmented pieces of preexisting larger land masses ("supercontinents").... According to the continental drift theory, the supercontinent Pangaea began to break up about 225 to 200 million years ago, eventually fragmenting into the continents as we know them today.
> (pubs.usgs.gov/gip/dynamic/historical.html)

> Pangaea is the concept that all of the land masses of the earth were at one time connected as one giant supercontinent. Looking at a world map, some of the continents look like they could fit together (Africa and South America, for example), like giant puzzle pieces. Does the Bible mention Pangaea? Not explicitly, but possibly. Genesis 1:9 records, "And God said, 'Let the water under the sky be gathered to one place, and let dry ground appear.' And it was so." Presumably, if all the water was "gathered to one place," the dry ground would also be all "in one place."
> (www.gotquestions.org/pangea-theory.html)

I believe the current world geography, which consists of many continents, is the by-product of the split of Pangaea, which was the result of the strong arm of God dealing with man once again after the Great Flood. Man had again incurred the wrath of God, which later required God to send a healing balm in the form of legions of ministering angels. The breakup of Pangaea devastated the population with death and life-threatening injuries requiring organ transplants and bone and tissue repair. The standing stones of Stonehenge, and other megalithic sites, were areas where the masses of people were healed of their injuries and various diseases by angels, who later began to make seasonal visits, as recorded in the Bible. I believe the truth about ancient stone monuments, such as Stonehenge and the Carnac Stones, is not about ancient man's ingenuity in construction but about his gratitude for what God did for him in order that he might continue to exist on the earth. This book will discuss periods of ancient and biblical histories to reveal the magnitude of angelic involvement in the preservation of man. The archaeological research of such men as John Parker Pearson (professor of archaeology), Timothy Darvil (professor of archaeology in the School of Conservation Sciences at Bournemouth University), and Geoff Wainwright (president of the Society of Antiquaries and chief archaeologist at English Heritage) were very influential in the development of my idea of mass healings by angels in ancient times.

The story of ancient stone monuments must be investigated the same way a detective would study multiple crime scenes. Each crime scene has evidence that leads to one crime. A failure to connect the scenes means that the crime might go unsolved. Each megalithic site has a story to tell that is part of a total story in stone. Ancient men strove to the limits of their capabilities and available resources to leave a message to future generations of their direct and widespread interactions with angels of God. They prepared grand displays like Stonehenge of England and the Carnac Stones of France that could not be ignored and would evoke enough questions to inspire diligent research into their meanings.

This book presents a nontraditional view of angels, who are often viewed as mystical winged creatures that can propel themselves at will through time and space. This view is possibly influenced by John's visions of an angel flying in heaven:

Revelation 14:6: And I saw another angel fly in the

midst of heaven, having the everlasting gospel to preach unto them that dwell on the earth.

But on earth, there are no Scriptures that refer to individual flight by angels. In contrast, there are the stories of an angel wrestling with Jacob until he was forced to bless him, angels that were hidden from the people by Lot in the cities of Sodom and Gomorrah, angels dispatched to pick up Elijah in a chariot of fire, and angels poised for Elisha's defense on a mountain in chariots of fire. These biblical stories raise the question as to why these angles did not fly.

2 Kings 2:11: And it came to pass, as they still went on, and talked, that, behold, there appeared a chariot of fire, and horses of fire, and separated them, and Elijah went up by a whirlwind.

2 Kings 6:17: And Elisha prayed, and said, "Lord, I pray thee, open his eyes, that he may see." And the Lord opened the eyes of the young man, and he saw; and, behold, the mountain was full of horses and chariots of fire round about Elisha.

We know from biblical studies that angels and the Holy Spirit are the task bearers of God, and angels are also powerful creatures who sometimes carry fiery swords to do battle for the children of God. But in the above Scriptures involving Elijah and Elisha, the word "angels" is not used. There are only references to horses and chariots. Are we to understand that the angels were riders or occupants of the horses and chariots of fire? In references to the horses and chariots of Pharaoh, there was an assumption that the horses and chariots had riders and drivers:

Exodus 14:7, 9: And he took six hundred chosen

chariots, and all the chariots of Egypt, and captains over every one of them. ... But the Egyptians pursued after them, all the horses and chariots of Pharaoh, and his horsemen, and his army, and overtook them encamping by the sea, beside Pihahiroth, before Baalzephon.

2 Kings 2:12: And Elisha saw it, and he cried, "My father, my father, the chariot of Israel, and its horsemen." And he saw him no more; and he took hold of his own clothes and tore them in two pieces.

Elisha cried out that he saw "horsemen" with the chariot of fire. Does this mean that he saw occupants of those chariots? This concept is an important factor in this book, which shows how angels used the "horses and chariots" to initiate a massive program of healing to save mankind after God allowed the supercontinent of Pangaea to separate in order to execute his judgment upon the rebellious people of Babel and the plains of Shinar.

# Chapter 1:   In the Garden with Adam and Eve

Genesis 2:15: And the Lord God took the man, and put him into the Garden of Eden to till it and to keep it.

Genesis 2:19: And out of the ground the Lord God formed every beast of the field, and every fowl of the air; and brought them unto Adam to see what he would call them: and whatsoever Adam called every living creature, that was the name thereof.

Genesis 3:7–9: And the eyes of them both were opened, and they knew that they were naked; and they sewed fig leaves together, and made themselves aprons. And they heard the voice of God walking in the garden in the cool of the day, and Adam and his wife hid themselves from the presence of the Lord God among the trees of the garden. And the Lord God called unto Adam and said, Where art thou?

Genesis 3:21: For Adam also and for his wife did the Lord God make coats of skin and clothed them.

> Genesis 3:24: So he drove out the man; and he placed at the east of the Garden of Eden cherubim.

Even though the Scriptures say the "Lord God," I believe they imply that an angel of God visited Adam and Eve while they were in the Garden of Eden. Genesis 3:8 says that Adam and Eve heard the voice of God walking in the garden. In order for Adam and Eve to hear the angel of God, that person had to produce a sound either by impressions on the ground, the rustling of the plants as he moved, the sound that he made within himself, or by a combination of all. The angel of God came to the garden for a personal contact with Adam and Eve and presented himself in a form they recognized. Adam and Eve hid after eating the forbidden fruit and realizing their nakedness. Their decision to hide seems to indicate that the angel of God had a humanlike characteristic of searching by visual scanning. Adam and Eve were called out from hiding, and the conversation that followed shows that Adam, Eve, and the angel of God spoke the same language. The consequences of their actions were explained to them, and they were subsequently expelled from the garden. Adam and Eve learned from the beginning that their disobedience changed their relationship with God and drastically altered their quality of life, which now included a plight upon the land on which they would live.

> Genesis 3:17–18: And unto Adam he said, Because thou hast hearkened unto the voice of thy wife, and hast eaten of the tree, of which I commanded thee, saying, Thou shalt not eat of it; cursed is the ground for thy sake; in sorrow shalt thou eat of it all the days of thy life; Thorns also and thistles shall it bring forth to thee; and thou shalt eat the herb of the field.

Genesis Chapter 2 and 3 indicate that even though Adam

and Eve were intelligent enough to till the ground and give names to the animals, they had limited resources in taking care of themselves after discovering their nakedness. They made aprons from fig leaves. The angel of God made coats of skin and clothed them with more appropriate clothing for their survival. Adam and Eve were sent from the Garden of Eden, but the clothing demonstrated God's desire for them to thrive. Genesis 3:24 uses the term "drove out" as though the expulsion was forceful, but the tailored clothes indicate that even though their actions mandated judgment and possibly destruction, God was willing to make provisions for their care. Along with discovering their nakedness, Adam and Eve also discovered their sensitivity to cold, heat, wind, and also the prickly nature of plants and the roughness of natural objects that could damage their skin. Their eyes and their senses were opened to the realities of the harshness of the natural world. As they began their journey into the world, there was hope that more help from God was forthcoming.

As Adam began his premier occupation as a tiller of the ground, he was subject to occupational hazards and injuries. In Genesis 3:19, God mentioned to Adam "the sweat of thy face," which indicated that his labor would be intense.

> Genesis 3:19: In the sweat of thy face shalt thou eat bread, till thou return unto the ground, for out of it wast thou taken; for dust thou art, and unto dust shalt thou return.

Health care became an important need as man embarked upon a life of demanding manual labor, a life that included the additional trauma of childbirth for Eve. Even though Adam and Eve were created with an ingrained intelligence, it is doubtful they had the knowledge to deal with the complexity of childbirth and postnatal care. The onset of pain for any reason, and the intense pain of childbirth in particular, must have been catastrophic issues. If we consider the fact that angels were given oversight of several highly significant biblical births such as Samson, John the Baptist, and Jesus Christ, we can surmise that the angels were surely given oversight of the birth of the first man born from a woman.

Genesis 4:1: And Adam knew Eve his wife: and she conceived, and bore Cain, and said, I have gotten a man from the Lord.

Judges 13:3: And the angel of the Lord appeared unto the woman, and said unto her, Behold, now, thou art barren, and bearest not; but thou shalt conceive, and bear a son [Samson].

Luke 1:13: And the angel said unto him, Fear not, Zacharias; for thy prayer is heard; and thy wife, Elisabeth, shall bear thee a son, and thou shalt call his name John.

Luke 1:31: And, behold, thou shalt conceive in thy womb, and bring forth a son, and shalt call his name Jesus.

The tone of Eve's voice in Genesis 4:1, as she announces her child, seems to be that of happiness and adulation to God, even after the pains of labor. Her statement, "I have gotten a man from the Lord," was not just a proclamation of the childbirth but also a hint of the process by which the child was delivered. It is possible that help from the angels of God gave Eve joy and also confidence in assuming this great responsibility. A successful delivery was important for the fulfillment of God's command to Adam and Eve to be fruitful and multiply. The joy and confidence of Eve and the success of the first family was contingent upon continuous obedience to God and angelic intervention.

I believe angels continued their direct involvement in the physical and emotional well-being of men, and their actions were later magnified to a great extent after the catastrophe of the split of Pangaea. The stone circles and many other ancient stone monuments are records of a prolonged period in which angels were intensely involved in ministering to mankind. This period of direct and intense involvement occurred because of God's chastisement of men due to their rebellion at the Tower of Babel. A host of angels was called upon to provide healing for the deep wounds of this great chastisement that destroyed and injured a great number of people. There was a shock to the birth/death ratio, which set man once again on the path to almost total extinction after the Great Flood of Noah's time.

# Chapter 2:    The Great
# Flood and Pangaea

One of the most devastating ancient catastrophic events studied by today's scientist is the separation of the continents. According to scientists, all continents were joined together as one land mass called Pangaea, and ruptures in the earth separated the supercontinent, which resulted in the current world geography. (Figure 1)

The Pangaea theory is one that states that all present continents were once together and collectively known as a supercontinent called Pangaea.
(The Pangaea Theory, library.thinkquest.org/17701/high/pangaea/)

The belief that continents have not always been fixed in their present positions was suspected long before the twentieth century; this notion was first suggested as early as 1596 by the Dutch map maker Abraham Ortelius in his work *Thesaurus Geographicus*. Ortelius suggested that the Americas were "torn away from Europe and Africa … by earthquakes and floods" and went on to say, "The vestiges of the rupture reveal themselves, if someone brings forward a map

of the world and considers carefully the coasts of the three [continents]."
(US Geological Survey, pubs.usgs.gov/gip/dynamic/historical.html)

I was rather surprised to find the following remarks in the journal *Nature*: We study our earth carefully; we shall see that everywhere it bears marks of having undergone a fearful catastrophe. Fossil substances, which originally belonged to the sea, have been found on the heights of mountains; the bones of animals have been discovered in countries the most remote from those they inhabit. Again, if we look at our maps, we shall see the parts of one continent that jut out, agree with the indented portions of another. The prominent coast of Africa would fit in the opposite opening between North and South America, and so in numerous other instances. A general rending asunder of the world would seem to have taken place.
(www.nature.com/nature/journal/v120/n3011/abs/120084d0.html)

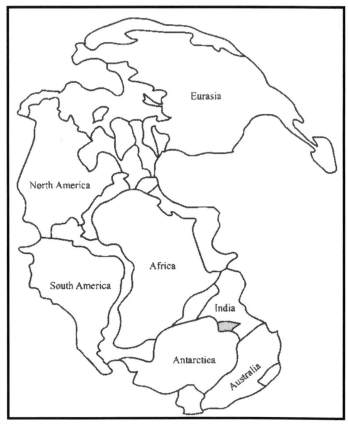

**Figure 1. Pangaea**

Some scientists believe that the model of Pangaea represents the world millions of years prior to the birth of mankind. This belief, in my opinion, requires an explanation of how man first emerged upon the earth. Scientific theories of evolution have been unsuccessful in establishing an initial timeline, or form, or fashion for the beginning of man. This book follows the indefinite but implied timeline given in the Book of Genesis in the Bible. Genesis records the creation of man as being close to the creation of the world. According to this understanding, I believe that man was present on the original world of the supercontinent of Pangaea. I believe that the model of Pangaea represents the world prior to, during, and immediately after the Great Flood of Noah's time. The Great Flood happened over the single continent of Pangaea.

The Great Flood over Pangaea marked the beginning of the conditions that became important factors in the separation of Pangaea into continents. Pangaea did not rupture silently. Since man was present on Pangaea prior to its separation, man was a victim of all the devastating effects of massive earthquakes and volcanoes associated with the separation of the land. The destruction upon the population of the earth was so great that it rivaled the Flood and required divine intervention by angels in a massive campaign of healing in order for man to continue upon the face of the earth.

The Bible states that, during the Great Flood, the fountains of the deep were broken up:

> Genesis 7:11: In the six hundredth year of Noah's life, in the second month, the seventeenth day of the month, the same day were all the fountains of the great deep broken up, and the windows of heaven were opened.

The Scriptures seem to support the idea of earthquakes and volcanic activities under water and on land. The events occurred in the deep or the ocean and caused humongous tsunamis to power their way to Pangaea from the east and the west, because Pangaea was one lateral land mass. The tsunamis from the east and from the west clashed at Pangaea, which caused the water to rise to the top of the mountains (Figure 2). Noah's Ark was perched safely at the top of Mount Ararat, but if the ark had not found refuge there, it would have been swept away by the clashing tsunamis and destroyed. God knew the impending violent raging of the waters so, according to the Scriptures, God sealed the door.

> Genesis 7:16: And they that went in, went in male and female of all flesh, as God had commanded him: and the Lord shut him in.

Some scientists speculate that during the flood, the land dropped well below sea level, or the sea floor rapidly rose, which accounts in part for the height of the water. If that is true, it is more conceivable that Pangaea dropped as a single land mass than that all of the areas of the current continental arrangement dropped individually. That would raise the question as to whether there is enough water in the ocean to cover all the mountains at the same time with the current world geography.

> There are many volcanic rocks interspersed between the fossil layers in the rock record—layers that were obviously deposited during Noah's flood. So it is quite plausible that these fountains of the great deep involved a series of volcanic eruptions with prodigious amounts of water bursting up through the ground. It is interesting that up to 70 percent or more of what comes out of volcanoes today is water, often in the form of steam.
> creation.com/images/pdfs/cabook/cha

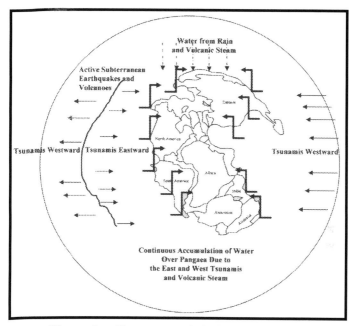

**Figure 2.  Pangaea and the Flood of Noah
(Drawing by the author)**

Earthquakes in the deep created tsunamis that traveled eastward and westward across Pangaea. The tsunamis continued until the earthquakes ceased. The earthquakes spawned subterranean volcanoes that spewed steam into the upper atmosphere, which condensed into rain.

In their catastrophic plate tectonics model for the flood, Austin et al. have proposed that at the onset of the flood, the ocean floor rapidly lifted up to 6,500 feet (2,000 meters) due to an increase in temperature as horizontal movement of the tectonic plates accelerated. This would spill the seawater onto the land and cause massive flooding—perhaps what is aptly described as the breaking up of the "fountains of the great deep." (www.christiananswers.net/q-aig/aig-c010.html)

The wave heights of the continuous clash of the tsunamis over Pangaea continued until the earthquakes and volcanic activities in the ocean ceased. It is possible that the earthquakes and volcanoes that caused the tsunamis of the Flood, along with the pounding of the massive weight of water against the land, caused great weaknesses in the foundation of the earth. These possible areas of geological weakness or fault lines were major factors in another cataclysmic event in the history of mankind involving the separation of Pangaea. It is important to understand the geography and timeline of Pangaea in order to fully understand the events at the Tower of Babel when God confounded the languages. I believe that the separation of Pangaea into continents began in the plains of Shinar during the time of the city of Babel. During the Flood, God brought judgment upon the unrighteous by allowing the rain to continue forty days and forty nights and the fountain of the deep to open. During the time of Shinar and the city of Babel, God brought judgment upon the people by allowing the initially benign faults in the earth to rupture as earthquakes and volcanoes formed on land. During the Flood, God purged the earth of the unrighteous people, and Noah and his family were left as the only survivors. But the generations of men reverted to their disobedience during the time of the city of Babel, which prompted God to impose upon them another catastrophe of immense proportion. God allowed the supercontinent of Pangaea to split, which created a worldwide scene of death and traumatic injuries. God then initiated a grand program of healing to save those who survived, and he did it by the dispatch of legions of angels. There was no other way mankind could survive.

# Chapter 3:   The Tower of Babel

Genesis 8:22: While the earth remaineth, seedtime and harvest, and cold and heat, and summer and winter, and day and night shall not cease.

Genesis 11:1–2: And the whole earth was of one language, and of one speech. And it came to pass, as they journeyed from the east, that they found a plain in the land of Shinar; and they dwelt there.

After the flood, civilization sprang up around the area of Mount Ararat, which was possibly located in the area that is presently called Asia. Since God said in Genesis 8:22 that the seasons would continue, winter might have influenced the masses to move to areas that were consistently warm and had abundant water supplies. The journey from the east might not be an indicator of the movement of a single mass of people but an indicator of a common direction to which the people migrated for a life change and to follow the leadership of Nimrod. The people settled in the Plain of Shinar, where they built the city of Babel and several other cities. The decision to concentrate the population in one area was contrary to God's request to Noah and his sons:

Genesis 9:1: And God blessed Noah and his sons,

and said unto them, Be fruitful and multiply, and fill the earth.

The people of Shinar were oblivious to the expectations of God because they were so in tune to the leadership of Nimrod. There was no one like Noah to admonish them to change their ways. It is doubtful that anyone would have heeded the saying of a righteous man because of the charisma of Nimrod.

Genesis 11:4: And they said, Come, let us build us a city and a tower, whose top may reach into heaven; and let us make us a name, lest we be scattered abroad upon the face of the whole earth.

Now it was Nimrod who excited them to such an affront and contempt of God. He was the grandson of Ham, the son of Noah, a bold man, and of great strength of hand. He persuaded them not to ascribe it to God, as if it were through his means they were happy, but to believe that it was their own courage which procured that happiness. He also gradually changed the government into tyranny, seeing no other way of turning men from the fear of God, but to bring them into a constant dependence on his power. He also said he would be revenged on God, if he should have a mind to drown the world again; for that he would build a tower too high for the waters to reach. And that he would avenge himself on God for destroying their forefathers. Now the multitude were very ready to follow the determination of Nimrod, and to esteem it a piece of cowardice to submit to God; and they built a tower. (from Josephus) (en.wikipedia.org/wiki/Nimrod)

History states there were six hundred thousand men working on the Tower of Babel, and the completion of the tower had precedence over individual life. Even pregnancy was considered less important than the completion of the tower. The arrogance of the people blinded their eyes to the possibility that God would impose punishment upon them for their actions and they would be powerless to prevent or withstand it. They would soon realize that the only salvation from an act of God is God.

> Six hundred thousand men (*Sefer ha-Yashar*, 12*a*) were engaged for forty-three years (Book of Jubilees, x) in building the Tower. The Tower had reached such a height that it took a whole year to hoist up necessary building-material to the top; in consequence, materials became so valuable that they cried when a brick fell and broke, while they remained indifferent when a man fell and was killed. They behaved also very heartlessly toward the weak and sick who could not assist to any great extent in the building; they would not even allow a woman in travail to leave.
> (*Jewish Encyclopedia*, www.jewishencyclopedia.com)

**Figure 3.   The Tower of Babel**
**en.wikipedia.org/wiki/Tower_of_Babel**

It was built of burnt brick, cemented together with mortar, made of bitumen, that it might not be liable to admit water.
en.wikipedia.org/wiki/Tower_of_Babel

And they began to build, and in the fourth week they made brick with fire, and the bricks served them for stone, and the clay with which they cemented them together was asphalt which comes out of the sea, and out of the fountains of water in the land of Shinar. (Jubilees 10:20–21, Charles' 1913 translation) (en.wikipedia.org/wiki/Tower_of_Babel)

Bitumen is a category of organic liquids which are highly viscous, black, sticky and wholly soluble in carbon disulfide. Asphalt and tar are the most common forms of bitumen. Natural bitumen could

be found in tar sands, coal, mud volcanoes, metallic ores, carbonaceous meteorites, igneous rocks, etc. The origin of bitumen probably is related to earth's mantle.
(Market Publishers, marketpublishers.com/ lists/1481/news.html)

The people of Shinar used at the tower a tarlike substance called bitumen that came from the sea and the fountains of the land. It is highly probable that the people who followed Nimrod moved from the east to an area rich in bitumen but near conditions favorable for earthquakes and volcanoes. The staging for earthquakes and volcanic activity were a result of the Great Flood and the tremendous pounding of Pangaea by the rising waters of the tsunamis.

The Tower of Babel was approximately a mile high, higher than the Eiffel Tower. Also, historians state that the base of the tower was like a mountain with spiral path wide enough to grow grain for the animals of labor. There had to be a great catastrophe to destroy such a structure. A catastrophe that devastated such a structure also devastated the population in the city of Babel and all other cities within a great radius of Babel.

The *Book of Jubilees* mentions the tower's height as being 5,433 cubits and 2 palms, or nearly 2.5 kilometers (about 1.55 miles). The *Third Apocalypse of Baruch* mentions that the "tower of strife" reached a height of 463 cubits (696 feet or 212 meters), taller than any structure built in human history until the construction of the Eiffel Tower (1,063 feet or 324 meters) in 1889.

The seventeenth-century historian Verstegan provides yet another figure: quoting Isidore, he says that the tower was 5,164 paces high, about 7.6 kilometers, and quoting Josephus that the tower was wider than it was high, more like a mountain than a tower. He also quotes unnamed authors who say that the spiral path was so wide that it contained lodgings for workers and animals, and other authors who claim that the path was wide enough to have fields for growing grain for the animals used in the construction. (en.wikipedia.org/wiki/Tower_of_Babel)

God observed the activities at the tower and determined that the people should be scattered "upon the face of all the earth." God intended for his actions to be thorough and permanent, so he instituted a threefold plan to ensure that man would be scattered throughout the world and be fruitful and multiply and fill the earth:

1. Confound the language
2. Separate the land of Pangaea
3. Change the physiology of man

Genesis 11:5–8: And the Lord came down to see the city and the tower, which the children of men builded. And the Lord said, Behold, the people are one, and they have all one language; and this they begin to do; and now nothing will be withheld from them, which they have imagined to do. Come, let us go down, and there confound their language, that they may not understand one another's speech. So the Lord scattered them abroad from there upon the face of all the earth; and they ceased building the city.

At the Tower of Babel, God confounded the speech and caused the development of many languages in order to destroy the unity and disperse the people, but the people attempted to continue in spite of conflicts from misunderstandings. The continuous confusion caused many deaths, and the project was abandoned.

> The confounding of the languages—before that they all had spoken Hebrew—then compelled them to give up the work, many also perishing on the occasion; for if any one received stones instead of mortar through the misunderstanding of his fellow-workers, he grew angry and threw the stones upon the one who had given them (*Sefer ha-Yashar*, 12*b*).
> (www.jewishencyclopedia.com/view.jsp?artid=45&letter=B&search=babel)

God then allowed the weaknesses in the foundation of the earth that developed during the Great Flood to rupture and begin the separation of the supercontinent of Pangaea. The earth ruptured, and the areas where the supply of bitumen was founded also spewed volcanic mixtures into the air. As the earth shook and the volcanic pressure bellowed upward, the destruction of the Tower of Babel began as the stones of the tower flailed outward in all directions for great distances. All stones that were not pulverized in the process of falling tumbled furiously across the landside and through the fleeing population. Many people perished in the tower upon its collapse, and many were lost when the base of the tower was swallowed by a great rift in the ground. The destruction of the tower by earthquakes and volcanoes began the development of dire worldwide conditions that threatened the survival of mankind.

The people of Babel and the surrounding areas who were fortunate enough to survive fled away in terror in all directions, but they found themselves victims of the split of Pangaea and isolated on newly formed continents that drifted farther and farther apart. The loss of countless lives and injuries were rampant on all of the emerging continents, especially along their borders. The mounting deaths and injuries called for a powerful rescue, but who had the resources to deal with a worldwide catastrophe? The people turned their cries toward heaven. The great movement of the earth and the deep rifts in the surface brought to their minds the destruction during the Great Flood because of the disobedience of their forefathers. Nimrod's threat against another flood from God was supplanted by the terror of earthquakes and volcanoes. The angels of heaven, with whom they were willing to wage war, became the recipients of their prayers for help.

Inhabitants stranded in the areas that are now Africa, North America, South America, and Asia had vast interiors in which to flee, but the inhabitants stranded in the area that became the United Kingdom were trapped in a confining area almost completely surrounded by water.

> The United Kingdom of Great Britain and Northern Ireland (commonly known as the United Kingdom, the UK, or Britain) … is an island country…. Northern Ireland is the only part of the UK with a land border, sharing it with the Republic of Ireland. Apart from this land border, the UK is surrounded by the Atlantic Ocean, the North Sea, the English Channel, and the Irish Sea. The largest island, Great Britain, is linked to France by the Channel Tunnel. (en.wikipedia.org/wiki/United_Kingdom)

The land was flooded on all sides of the rift on all continents during the formation of the new Atlantic Ocean, and the flooding was a threat to God's promise to Noah that he would not destroy all flesh by a flood again.

> Genesis 9:15: And I will remember my covenant, which is between me and you and every living creature

of all flesh; and the waters shall no more become a flood to destroy all flesh.

With so many people dying, divine intervention was imperative. The future propagation of mankind was bleak, because man had no way of surviving on his own. The population was in dire need of physical and emotional healing. As the natural catastrophe occurred, the confusion of the languages contributed greatly to the mounting death toll. Many men, women, and children lay in misery and were incapable of soliciting the help of anyone but God through agonizing prayers.

The transformation of the land continued as the climate quickly deteriorated, and the land became like a tomb of cold darkness. The earthquakes and the rifts spawned volcanoes, and the volcanoes unleashed great clouds of ash and steam over the world. The sunlight was blocked, which resulted in a sudden and rapid plunge in the global temperature. The tattered survivors, especially in the secluded United Kingdom, watched as the waters cooled and congealed to form valleys of ice. The sudden temperature change was characteristic of examples in recent centuries of the effect of volcanic action on the climatic temperature.

The eastern U.S. recorded the lowest-ever winter average temperature in 1783–84, about 4.8°C below the 225-year average. Europe also experienced an abnormally severe winter. Benjamin Franklin suggested that these cold conditions resulted from the blocking out of sunlight by dust and gases created by the Iceland Laki eruption in 1783. The Laki eruption was the largest outpouring of basalt lava in historic times. Franklin's hypothesis is consistent with modern scientific theory, which suggests that large volumes of SO$_2$ are the main culprit in haze-effect global cooling.

Thirty years later, in 1815, the eruption of Mount Tambora, Indonesia, resulted in an extremely cold spring and summer in 1816, which became known as the *year without a summer*. The Tambora eruption is believed to be the largest of the last ten thousand years. New England and Europe were hit exceptionally hard. Snowfalls and frost occurred in June, July, and August, and all but the hardiest grains were destroyed. Destruction of the corn crop forced farmers to slaughter their animals. Soup kitchens were opened to feed the hungry. Sea ice migrated across Atlantic shipping lanes, and alpine glaciers advanced down mountain slopes to exceptionally low elevations. (www.geology.sdsu.edu/how_volcanoes_work/climate_effects.html)

The ice formation during the separation of the land was a different result than what occurred during the Great Flood of Noah's time. During the Flood, the water was of a much greater magnitude and in constant motion across Pangaea, which prevented the water from freezing. When the water abated, Noah was soon able to prepare the land for agriculture after a period of rapid global warming.

Genesis 9:20: And Noah began to be a farmer; and he planted a vineyard.

But the victims of the continental separations were faced with freezing water that eventually congealed to ice, and they had no ark in which to await the climatic change necessary for survival. The climate continued to deteriorate while they were in the midst of an evolving catastrophe that seemed to have no end.

Earth is sometimes pictured as a world in free motion to evolve as it will, and the fate of man is seen as governed by his resilience and good fortune in surviving. However, the resilience and good fortune of man was hardly adequate for survival when the single land mass split into continents and caused mass deaths and injuries. God was well aware of man's afflictions and did not sit idly by while man progressed toward inevitable extinction. God had at his command armies of angels that were capable of providing whatever was needed for man's survival.

It was previously mentioned that God allowed the faults in the earth to rupture because of the rebellious people at the Tower of Babel. God's judgment was firm as it is often displayed in the books of the Bible. He doesn't withhold his judgment because of the potential for death and suffering among the people. Consider his judgment against the families of Korah, Dathan, and Abiram in the Book of Numbers. Moses declared God's judgment and the earth executed it:

> Numbers 16:30–33: But if God makes a new thing, and the earth open her mouth and swallow them up, with all that appertains unto them, and they go down alive into the pit; then ye shall understand that these men have provoked the Lord. And it came to pass, as he had finished speaking all these words, that the ground split open that was under them; And the earth opened its mouth, and swallowed them up, and their houses, and all the men that appertained unto Korah, and all their goods. They, and all that appertained to them, went down alive into the pit, and the earth closed upon them; and they perished from among the congregation.

The story in the Book of Numbers illustrates God's judgment upon a selected group of people and his use of a selected area of the ground to fulfill that judgment. The congregation of his people was shaken up by the deaths and brought back together again with an understanding of what had occurred and why. The Tower of Babel involved the world population incorporated into one unified act of defiance to God. The judgment of God was inflicted upon the total population, and God prepared for their restoration through angelic healings.

God listened to the cries of the people of the world, especially in the United Kingdom, and he answered with an immense dispatch of angels. Angels came swiftly in their "horses and chariots of fire" as described in Elijah's experience in the Book of 2 Kings. They came in tens of thousands to launch a worldwide campaign of physical and emotional healing. They saw the faces of desperate people who were reaching out and expressing their agony in their languages. The angels began a healing campaign that was initiated in the United Kingdom, where the rate of death exceeded that of other parts of the world due to its isolation. The campaign was primarily concentrated around all the coastal areas of the United Kingdom and extended to the coastal areas of Africa and the new worlds of the Americas. The coastal areas were of primary concern because much of the land mass from the coast and miles inward was covered with freezing water and ice.

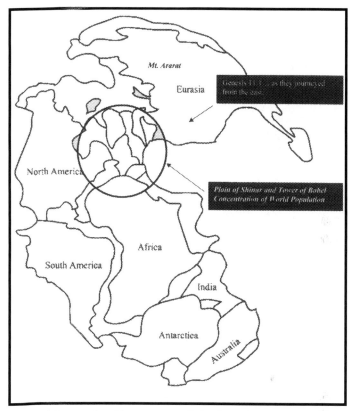

**Figure 4.    Pangaea and the Land of Shinar**
**(Map outline from en.wikivisual.com/index.php/Pangaea)**
**(Enhancements by the author)**

It is important to discuss at this point the timeline for the destruction of the Tower of Babel and the split of Pangaea. The Book of Genesis gives reference to the division of the earth during the time of a man named Peleg:

> Genesis 10:25: And unto Eber were born two sons; the name of one was Peleg, for in his days was the earth divided; his brother's name was Joktan.

Four generations after Noah, Genesis 10:25 records the birth of Peleg (meaning *division*) "for in his days was the earth divided." Some suggest the continents of the earth were divided at this time. However, this seems unlikely; as such a process would have had to occur within a very confined time period. The resultant geological violence would be overwhelmingly catastrophic—like another Noahic Flood all over again. Any continental separation thus likely occurred *during* the Flood.
(www.answersingenesis.org/creation/v22/i1/peleg.asp)

Further, God is capable of expediting the continental drift process to accomplish His goal of separating humanity (Genesis 11:8). Again, though, the Bible does not explicitly mention Pangaea, or conclusively tell us when Pangaea was broken apart.
(www.gotquestions.org/pangea-theory.html)

I believe that the association of the division of the earth with Peleg is a literary choice of the writer because the name Peleg means "division." The chronology of families in chapter 10 is followed by historical activities in Chapter 11, thus there is a close association of the time of Peleg to the time of the Tower of Babel.

Genesis 10:20: These are the sons of Ham, after their families, after their tongues, in their countries, and in their nations.

Genesis 10:31–32: These are the sons of Shem, after their families, after their tongues, in their lands, after their nations. These are the families of the sons of Noah, after their generations, in their nations; and by these were the nations divided in the earth after the Flood.

Genesis 11:9: Therefore is the name of it called Babel, because the Lord did there confound the language of all the earth; and from there did the Lord scatter them abroad upon the face of the earth.

Surely the sons of Noah spoke the same language after exiting the Ark after the Flood, but Genesis chapter 10 refers to "after their tongues, in their land, after their nation." Genesis chapter 11 says the people were scattered after the confusion of languages, which means that the families divided according to their tongues, in their lands and after their nation, after the Tower of Babel event and after, I believe, the split of Pangaea.

# Chapter 4:    The Glitter of Hope

Angels are powerful and dreadful, endowed with wisdom and with knowledge of all earthly events, correct in their judgment, holy, but not infallible; for they strive with each other, and God has to make peace between them. When their duties are not punitive, angels are beneficent to man.
www.fact-index.com/a/an/angel.html

Revelation 5:11: And I beheld, and I heard the voice of many angels round about the throne and the living creatures, and the elders, and the number of them was ten thousand times ten thousand, and thousands of thousands.

The thought of armies or legions of angels on earth involved in preventing the extinction of mankind is a lot to consider. However, the duties and number of angels employed for any reason is in proportion to the task to be performed. Elijah was taken up by one "chariot of fire" because he was a single individual. If there had been a thousand men to be taken up, more chariots of fire of the same size would have arrived. When Jesus was born, there was a heavenly host praising God, which implies many angels. When Jesus was in the process of being arrested in the Garden of Gethsemane, he stated he could call more than twelve legions of angels to his rescue. The

Scriptures say that Enoch prophesized that Jesus will return with ten thousand of his saints. And Jacob saw the Lord's host on earth, which implies many angels. So the idea of a crowd of angels on earth at one time is biblically acceptable. Events on earth dictate the number.

Luke 2:13: And suddenly there was with the angel a multitude of the heavenly host, praising God.

Matthew 26:53: Thinkest thou that I cannot now pray to my Father, and he shall presently give me more than twelve legions of angels?

Jude 1:14–15: And Enoch also, the seventh from Adam, prophesied of these, saying, "Behold, the Lord cometh with ten thousands of his saints To execute judgment upon all."

2 Kings 6:17: And Elisha prayed, and said, Lord, I pray thee, open his eyes, that he may see. And the Lord opened the eyes of the young man, and he saw; and behold, the mountain was full of horses and chariots of fire round about Elisha.

Genesis 32:1: And Jacob went on his way, and the angels of God met him. And when Jacob saw them, he said, this is God's host: and he called the name of that place Mahanaim.

Host—a very large number.
(*Webster's Ninth New Collegiate Dictionary*)

The people in the United Kingdom saw the arrival of "horses and chariots of fire" that descended from the sky, just as the people in the Bible saw when Elijah was taken up to heaven. The people in Elijah's time saw only a few vehicles, but the people in the United Kingdom saw numerous vehicles arrive and descend because of the magnitude of the task to be performed. A multitude of people lay injured and dying, with no hope of medical care and rescue. The angels arrived in circular chariots of fire, as symbolized by the Stonehenge monument (Figure 5). Stonehenge was constructed to show that the people saw objects whose circular shapes were formed by a series of columns with spaces, containing unknown material between each column. It was beyond their ability to depict what was in the spaces between the columns because the spaces contained material such as glass or other reflective surface or lights that could not be depicted in stone. The unknown materials between the columns are symbolized at Stonehenge by the presence of the lintels in conjunction with the standing stones. The lintels indicate an attempt to frame spaces as one would frame windows, doorways, or gateways. The ancient people were not familiar with glass or any other reflective material or lights.

It might seem absurd to write of strange vehicles coming to earth, but the prehistoric men saw something which they tried to relay in stone. A project constructed so large with no obvious practical purpose seems to imply there was an observation by the masses, which they agreed was worthy of memorializing.

It was previously mentioned in the introduction that the monuments at the stone circles and other megalithic sites must be investigated similar to a crime with multiple crime scenes. Each scene contains valuable information for solving the one crime. The ancient people built Stonehenge to show the basic design of the chariots of fire that arrived, and the megalithic sites called "medicine wheels" in North America provide insight to an important feature of the chariots of fire.

**Figure 5.    Stonehenge Enhancement**
**Drawing by the author**

There are spaces between the stones because the material that connected the columns of the object was of a transparent nature such as glass, or there were lights. There was nothing that could simulate transparency or artificial light, so the spaces were left open.

The inner and outer circles are possibly representative of a two-tiered structure rather than a single level structure.

The top view is represented by the small inner circle. Men were not able to depict in stone the glasslike circular top that protruded upward from the main circular frame. They did enough to show that there was a small inner structure in the middle of the larger outer circle.

The choice of the stones with the smooth surface is possibly an indication that the object had a framework that appeared to be smooth such as a metallic surface.

Was the arrangement of the stones, which allowed the penetration of the sun at a certain angle or level, intended to re-create the light that was in or around the object? Men had no other way to symbolize artificial light and possibly believe that the light in the object was caused by the sun or was even a portion of the sun. The stones represent the framework of a circular object.

The volcanic activities during the rift of Pangaea darkened the sky by blocking out the sunlight; however, the efforts of the angels were enhanced by artificial lighting from the transporters, which the ancient people of North America depicted through their medicine wheels (Figure 6). They were also in perilous conditions, and they were visited by the chariots of fire and constructed stonework to memorialize their observations.

Medicine wheels, or sacred hoops, were constructed by laying stones in a particular pattern on the ground. Most medicine wheels follow the basic pattern of having a center of stone(s), and surrounding that is an outer ring of stones with "spokes," or lines of rocks, radiating from the center. Some ancient types of sacred architecture were built by laying stones on the surface of the ground in particular patterns common to aboriginal peoples.

Medicine wheels appear all over northern United States and southern Canada, specifically South Dakota, Wyoming, Montana, Alberta, and Saskatchewan. Most of the wheels have been found in Alberta. In all over seventy medicine wheels have been found.

The most common deviation between different wheels is the spokes. There is no set number of spokes for a medicine wheel to have. The spokes within each wheel are rarely evenly spaced out, or even all the same length. Some medicine wheels will have one particular spoke that's significantly longer than the rest, suggesting something important about the direction it points.

An odd variation sometimes found in medicine wheels is the presence of a passageway, or a doorway, in the circles. The outer ring of stones will be broken, and there will be a stone path leading up to the center of the wheel.

(Medicine Wheels, Crystalinks, www.crystalinks.com/medicinewheel.html)

Archaeologists have not derived a clear theory of the reason for the construction of the medicine wheels, but I see in the variations of the circular patterns the depiction of fluctuating and possibly rotating light sources that appear to be similar to the rotating lights of lighthouses. As we view the beacon of a lighthouse, the lengths of the beams vary as they approach and rotate away from our position. The people saw the chariots of fire with artificial light sources that were indeed wonders to them, and the extension of each beam of light was considered an individual wonder. The wonders made things bright as they cut through the darkness near the people.

The above description notes a variation in the patterns of the medicine wheels, with a stone pathway to the center of some of the monuments. This seems to indicate that an entranceway for the chariot of fire was opened and the light from the interior cast a beam to the ground on the outside. The beam of light from the entranceway appeared to be a wide pathway to the chariot of fire. As the angels exited, they appeared to walk on the glowing pathway as the exterior lights of the chariots of fire rotated around the area. I believe the people made observations over a lengthy period of time, and Figure 6 shows the chariots of fire's lights in several modes of operation: exterior and interior lights on, interior lights on and exterior lights off, exterior and interior lights off (as illustrated by the completely dark circular pattern). The medicine wheels appear to be views of the chariots of fire from heights. It is possible that the people of North America went to the mountains to avoid the rising waters and to escape the aftershocks of the earthquakes that split Pangaea.

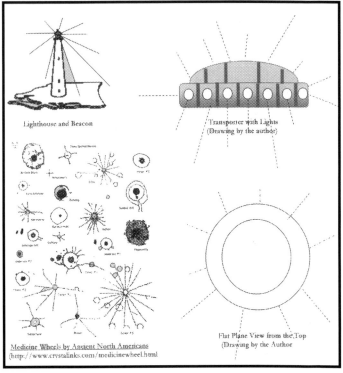

Lighthouse and Beacon

Transporter with Lights
(Drawing by the author)

Medicine Wheels by Ancient North Americans
(http://www.crystalinks.com/medicinewheel.html

Flat Plane View from the Top
(Drawing by the Author

**Figure 6.    Medicine Wheels of North America**

As the chariots of fire appeared in the sky, the people were moaning and crying out in the confusion of their languages in the cold darkness. Some walked, stumbled, and crawled on top of each other in a disoriented manner in an attempt to move farther from the rapidly rising and freezing waters; however; in the United Kingdom there was nowhere to go. Many lay in anticipation of death. They suddenly saw glowing objects descend from the sky with their streaks of daylight, which illuminated the area. It was as though God had descended in person upon the people to issue out punishment for their continuous disobedience. They offered up pleas of mercy in the variety of their tongues as they waited in expectation of more judgment and death. Instead of judgment, they began to feel the rumbling of the ground as the chariots of fire began to remove vast quantities of dirt and ice from the ground during the construction of circular ditches at the landing sites. The angels knew that the energy from their chariots of fire, the same energy that created the swirl around Elijah in the Bible, would melt the ice and send broken pieces of ice and water outward toward the people. So, the ditches and the external banks were constructed to contain the water and ice and to eventually provide ground upon which they and the people could walk. If the ditches and external banks were not constructed, it would have been necessary for the rescuers and victims to tread through high water and ice while traveling to and from the chariots of fire. The external banks were also constructed to prevent any ice that melted in the surrounding hillsides from draining into the ditch and flooding the land around the transporters (Figure 7).

The force by which the water and the melting ice were channeled to the ditches was greater than the energy from the fiery chariot that caused the whirlwind when it came for Elijah.

2 Kings 2:11: And it came to pass, as they still went on, and talked, that, behold, there appeared a chariot of fire, and horses of fire, and separated them, and Elijah went up by a whirlwind into heaven.

Whirlwind—a small rotating windstorm of limited extent marked by an inward and upward spiral motion of the lower air that is followed by an outward and upward spiral motion.
(*Webster's Ninth New Collegiate Dictionary*)

The report of a whirlwind around Elijah is an indicator that the chariot or vessel that arrived had some type of onboard circular motion as it hovered over him. The spiraling of the sand around Elijah was as the spiraling of the water and ice outward to the ditch at Stonehenge. The construction of the circular ditches required the volume of dirt to be relocated somewhere in the region, thus, the Sillsbury Hill (Figure 8) was created which, according to archaeologist reports, is an ancient man-made hill of unknown purpose. If the chariot of fire in the Bible was able to lift up Elijah for transport away from the area, it was also capable of lifting up and transporting dirt away from an area such as Stonehenge to the artificial mound of Sillsbury Hill.

**Figure 7.    Stonehenge: Ditch and Embankment**
**Embankment around the Stone Circle**
**(www.crystalinks.com/stonehenge.html)**

**Figure 8.    Sillsbury Hill**
www.essentially-england.com/prehistoric-england.html

Sillsbury Hill, located just south of the village of Avebury in Wiltshire, is a massive artificial mound with a flat top. It is approximately 130 feet (40 meters) high, with a base circumference of 1,640 feet. It is composed of over 12 million cubic feet (339,600 cubic meters) of chalk and earth and covers over 5 acres.
(witcombe.sbc.edu/earthmysteries/EMSilbury.html)

Composed mainly of chalk and clay excavated from the surrounding area, the mound stands 40 meters (130 feet) high and covers about 5 acres (2 hectares). It is a display of immense technical skill and prolonged control over labour and resources. Archaeologists calculate that Sillsbury Hill was built about 4,750 years ago and that it took 18 million man-hours, or 500 men working 15 years (Atkinson 1974:128) to deposit and shape 248,000 cubic meters (324,000 cubic yards) of earth and fill on top of a natural hill. Euan W. Mackie asserts that no simple late Neolithic tribal structure as usually imagined could have sustained this and similar projects, and envisages an authoritarian theocratic power elite with broad-ranging control across southern Britain. (www.malmesbury.com/things-to-do-further-afield/218-silbury-hill.html)

The volume of dirt at Sillsbury Hill is estimated at twelve million cubic feet. I believe that the estimated volume of Sillsbury Hill matches the estimated total volume of all the ditches that are associated with the megalithic sites in the United Kingdom. The phenomenon is no different than at modern construction sites where large holes are dug and mounds appear. The latter part of the above descriptions of Sillsbury Hill states that archaeologists believe the work was supervised by "an authoritarian theocratic power with broad-ranging control across southern Britain."

Theocratic (theocracy)—government of a state by immediate divine guidance or by officials who are regarded as divinely guided.
(*Webster's Ninth New Collegiate Dictionary*)

The construction of Sillsbury Hill was not just a project under the supervision of divine authority but also a product of divine labor. It was an important orderly preparation of the area for the massive healing program across the world.

The relocation of the dirt to Sillsbury Hill was obviously not done by hand. Human beings are not heavy enough to pack a mound of dirt to that height. In modern construction, the dirt is packed down by heavy machinery that is driven over it. The chariots of fire applied weight to the top of the mound at certain intervals for the same reason. Each application of weight would flatten the top of the mound and make it appear to have terraces or spiraling pathways. The final dump and application of weight would leave a mound with a flat top as described above: "Sillsbury Hill, located just south of the village of Avebury in Wiltshire, is a massive artificial mound with a flat top."

And what is the purpose of a man-made hill, in a landscape full of natural ones?
(Sillsbury Hill, www.essentially-england.com/ prehistoric-england.html)

The above question from the Essentially England website is a very interesting one. The angels may have wanted to disguise a hill constructed by them in the midst of the natural hills, or perhaps they wanted to maintain the integrity of the landscape by not scattering the dirt throughout the area. Also, the huddled crowds of people could have made it difficult to spread the dirt in the immediate areas around the ditches. A central location appears to be the best solution. Sillsbury Hill is the answer to those of us who would ask, "What happened to the dirt from the ditches around Stonehenge and other sites?"

The ditches were capable of retaining a tremendous volume of water, and a simple volume calculation can give an idea of their capacities. Circular ditches were common to Stonehenge, Avebury, and the Ring of Brogar in the United Kingdom and at the Goseck Circle in Germany. Figure 7 shows the ring at Stonehenge, and Figure 9 shows the water capacity calculations for the ditch at the Ring of Brogar.

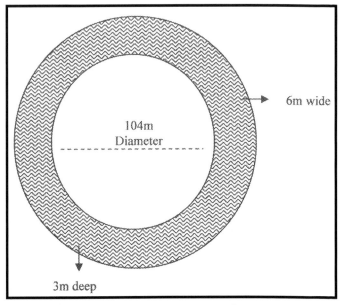

**Figure 9.   Example of the Water Capacities of a Circular Ditch**
**Ring of Brogar, Great Britain: 104 meters in diameter, 6 meters wide, and 3 meters deep**

Total volume in feet (1 meter = 3.28 feet):

104 meters + 6 meters + 6 meters = 116 meters = 380.48 feet for the diameter of the outer ring of the ditch
104 meters = 341.12 feet for the diameter of the inner ring of ditch
Volume of the outer ring = 8,390,912 gallons
Volume of the inner ring = 6,744,656 gallons
Volume of the ditch = volume of outer ring 8,390,912 – volume of inner ring 6,744,656

Capacity of the ditch = 1,646,256 gallons

Volume calculations per Circular Shaped Pond Calculator, www.geocheminc.com/circlecalc.htm

An archaeological report of the stone circle at Avebury states the belief that the ditch around the stone circle was once filled with water. I believe the report is correct and supports the idea of water retention.

The excavation of the encircling ditch required an estimated 200,000 tons of rock to be chipped and scraped away with the crudest of stone tools and antler picks (there is some evidence that this ditch was once filled with water, thereby giving the inner stone rings the appearance of being set upon an island. (Avebury, England, www.sacredsites.com/europe/england/avebury.html)

Archaeologist believe that the ditches around Stonehenge and other prehistoric sites were built by the ancient people using deer antlers. The ditches measured approximately 320 feet in diamenter and 36 feet deep.

The native Neolithic people of England began construction of Stonehenge I by digging a circular ditch using deer antlers as picks. The circle is 320 feet in diameter, and the ditch itself was 20 feet wide and 7 feet deep.
(www.sacred-destinations.com/england/stonehenge)

The site was surveyed and excavated intermittently between 1908 and 1922 by a team of workmen under Harold St. George Gray. He was able to demonstrate that the Avebury builders had dug down 11 meters (36 feet) into the natural chalk in excavating the henge

> ditch, producing an outer bank 9 meters (30 feet) high
> around the whole perimeter of the henge and using
> red deer antler as their primary digging tool. (www.
> crystalinks.com/avebury.html)

> It has been estimated that the ditch was about 30
> feet deep and was dug out of the underlying chalk
> using antlers for pick axes and ox shoulder blades for
> shovels. And once piled up, the excavated soil would
> have produced a 55-foot-high bank.
> (www.essentially-england.com/avebury.htm)

Some archaeologists believe two conflicting ideas: the ancient men dug such massive pits with deer antlers, and they moved massive stones many miles to build monuments. It seems that those who were ingenious enough to devise a way to move and assemble massive stones could have also fashioned more efficient tools for digging. I don't believe antlers were used for digging, and considering the size of the ditches, there should have been evidence of hundreds or even thousands of antler picks at the sites. And, of course, there is the question of how did men make a perfect circle of such size while digging with antler picks. Also, if we believe in the biblical story of Adam, Eve, Cain, and Abel, we understand that Adam was given the ability to till the ground, Cain was a hunter, and Abel was a farmer. All three men needed tools of labor. If the men of the first family were able to complete their work using tools, why were the men of the megalithic era so lacking in efficient tools? There should have been a natural progression toward better and better tools of labor. If those tools were used to build the ditches, those tools would have been found.

The victims of the collapse of the Tower of Babel and the split of Pangaea were in no physical or mental condition to consider digging a common pit. All of their energy was applied to basic survival – food, water, and shelter. They had lost family members and friends, and many were clinging to life. There was little or no collective strength as was shown at the Tower of Babel. Only the angels had the need and the ability to construct the ditches.

# Chapter 5:    The Procession

As previously mentioned, the total story of the stone circles and other megalithic sites must be put together as evidence in a crime with multiple crime scenes. There is Stonehenge, which depicts the chariots of fire; the medicine wheels, which illustrate the lights of the chariots of fire; the ditches, which are the indicators of the power and circular motion aboard the chariots of fire; the artificial Sillsbury Hill; and the Carnac Stones of France (Figure 10). I believe the Carnac Stones give an idea of the procession of angels that exited the chariots of fire to aid the victims of the split of Pangaea. The precision exhibited in the construction of perfect circular ditches at Stonehenge and other sites are indicative of a total concept of order and perfection. The procession of angels from the transporters, in my opinion, reflected the same concept. The arrangement of the Carnac Stones indicates that the angels exited in formation, as viewed by the people who created the stone monuments.

**Figure 10. Carnac Stones and the Procession**
(www.crystalinks.com/carnacstones.html)
**The Procession by the author and artist David Lang**

Carnac and its neighboring villages still hold in the region of 4,000 megalithic stones. Archaeologists believe that the original amount was probably close to 10,000 stones.
(www.philipcoppens.com/carnac.html)

All three fields are constructed on the same principle:

45

the tallest stones are located on the western side; the western side is also situated on higher ground than its eastern counterpart. The smaller stones on the eastern side are also at smaller intervals from each other. The rows also slightly spread out.

The stone row of Menec is the end of the series of stone rows.... Once again, we find that the tallest stand (stones) are standing on the highest ground.
(Counting Stones, www.philipcoppens.com/carnac.html)

The twelve parallel rows were graded in height starting with the largest stones at the west (the village end), decreasing in height until the alignment terminates at another "egg-shaped" circle. The stones are not only graded along the alignments, but *across them* too, which suggests an amount of planning and preparation took place before the stones were positioned and that they were selected according to some criteria, which we can only now guess at.
(www.ancient-wisdom.co.uk/francecarnac.htm)

The people saw the angels exit at a distance and move toward them in formation, so the angels who were closer were viewed as being of equal height, and those who were in the distance were viewed as being shorter. In order to give as accurate an account possible, tall stones were placed on higher ground. The distances between the stones are greater near the taller stones because as the angels approached them, the gap between them was more discernible. Such details were important to the creators of the Carnac Stones because the event was such a magnificently memorable one.

An important prerequisite in any emergency operation is an orderly and tactical dispersion of personnel and resources.

The number of injured people required a wide and far-reaching dispersion in order to ensure immediate help to the most critical persons. The people, who were once rebellious and victims of the collapse of the Tower of Babel and the split of Pangaea, or what they perceived to be the end of the world, became recipients of the outpouring of the mercy of God. Legions of angels came to minister to their pains and sufferings. The Carnac Stones are round because the people saw a symphony of angels bending over and kneeling to help in the gloom of the day and the darkness of the night. They moved among the bodies to reach those who were still alive and provided immediate medical care. Those who were in need of critical surgeries were taken to chariots of fire and other spaces for treatment.

The efforts to get the most critically injured people to the healing spaces were very tedious because of the darkness over the land. The angels had to eventually establish a sense of direction for themselves and the inhabitants. For instance, the chariots of fire were circular; how does a person enter a circular building or vessel? If all sides look the same, the entrance to anything circular has to be clearly defined. So, special stones had to be erected, as in Figure 7, at the entrance, just as it is done in modern-day signage. If there are multiple entrances, each entrance of like function will receive similar signage. The tall entrance stones seem odd standing in their places today, because the circular objects with the entranceways to which they belonged have departed. They stand now only as stones set apart from a symbolic stone circle.

In addition to the standing stones, the angels used chalk and gypsum to line the routes to the healing areas. These routes are called avenues by today's archaeologists. The chalk and gypsum were florescent in the night and the gloom of day, which expedited movement to and from the chariots of fire.

Archaeological excavation of the central henge [in

47

Thornborough] has taken place. It has been suggested that its banks were covered with locally mined gypsum. The resulting white sheen would have been striking and visible for miles around. A double alignment of pits, possibly evidence of a timber processional avenue, extends from the southern henge.
(www.crystalinks.com/thornborough.html)

The description of the avenue at Thornborough can be applied to Stonehenge and other megalithic sites. There is an abundant presence of chalk and gypsum.

There was a continuous procession of angels and the injured and dying moving along the avenues, over the retention ditches, through the standing stone entranceways, and to the chariots of fire and other spaces. As the angels transported the incapacitated, others began to follow them with their own strength. It is impossible to know the number of people who were in the processions across the world, but more than one thousand stone circles have been record along the coast of Great Britain. If each was a satellite of the healing program, then there were a great number of people needing care just in England.

More than one thousand stone circles have been cataloged for the British Isles and parts of Western Europe, most lying not more than a hundred miles from the sea.
(en.wikipedia.org/wiki/Stone_circle)

The population of Shinar can be estimated at several million minimally, if we consider that six hundred thousand men were assigned to work on the tower at one time. That number was a part of the total population, which included the women, children, leaders of the cities of Shinar, farmers, craftsmen, hunters, the elderly and disabled, and any other who was not assigned or capable of working at the tower. The urgency of building probably mandated more than one shift of workers. The urgency for medical care after the split of Pangaea mandated a round-the-clock treatment program.

The angels were able to communicate with the masses whose tongues were confounded at the Tower of Babel because they were part of the process by which the languages were confounded. The universal language spoken by the angels greatly benefited the rescue operation. The people who would have had great fear in seeing strange flying vessels with lights began to reach out to the strange occupants who spoke their languages. The Bible indicates in its report of the Day of Pentecost that the spirit of God is capable of speaking all languages simultaneously. Angels are ministering spirits and messengers of God.

> Acts 2:7–8: And they were all amazed and marveled, saying one to another, "Behold, are not all these who speak Galileans? And how hear we every man in our own tongue, wherein we were born?"

What a horribly traumatic yet immensely glorious time it was! The rebellious people, who were bewildered by the confusion of their languages and then traumatized by the separation of Pangaea, found themselves in unimaginable agony from injuries while trying to escape rising and freezing water. After waiting on death, they were in the company of angels. They moved through illuminated avenues en route to a huge glowing object and to the healing spaces, where they enter maimed and broken and exited whole.

# Chapter 6:    Trauma Care

Two of Britain's leading archaeologists, both world-renowned experts on Stonehenge, think they may have finally solved the riddle of the great standing stones. Professor Timothy Darvil and Professor Geoff Wainwright are not convinced, as others have been, that Stonehenge was a holy place or a secular tool for calculating dates. Instead, they think Stonehenge was a site of healing.

The bones that have been excavated from around Stonehenge appear to back the theory up. "There's an amazing and unnatural concentration of skeletal trauma in the bones that were dug up around Stonehenge," says Darvil. "This was a place of pilgrimage for people ... coming to get healed." (www.bbc.co.uk/history/programmes/stonehenge/article1.shtml) (www.bbc.co.uk/history/programmes/stonehenge/biographies.shtml)

I am convinced that Professors Darvil and Wainwright are indeed accurate in their assessment of Stonehenge as a site of healing. I also believe that the concept of healing goes much farther than their report. Men in general have a tendency to avoid spiritual or biblical explanation of mysterious events and often strain to explain them exclusively within secular boundaries. The healing that took place at Stonehenge was of God and initiated for the survival of mankind. There are no details in the Bible or ancient secular records, because no one was spared the horrible devastation. The people were in need of immediate care for traumatic injuries due to the earthquakes, volcanoes, rising and freezing waters, and starvation. The angels did not come to prepare records but to minister by providing emotional and physical healing.

The victims of the continental rifts, volcanoes, flooding, and freezing temperature presented a wide variety of injuries that needed immediate advance trauma care. Successful trauma care involves the process of repairing, removing, and replacing damaged body parts. The extent of the worldwide injuries and death is not actually known, but the reports of modern-day earthquakes such as the Haitian earthquake of 2010 can give us a glimpse of the worldwide medical conditions during the division of Pangaea. Each description of the conditions in Haiti must be multiplied many times to give the understanding of the conditions in Pangaea.

The 7.0-magnitude quake killed an estimated 200,000 people, according to Haitian government figures cited by the European Commission. The U.N. said Saturday the government had preliminarily confirmed 111,481 bodies, but that figure does not account for corpses buried by relatives.
(Yahoo! News, news.yahoo.com/s/ap/20100123/ ap_on_re_la_am_ca/cb_haiti_earthquake)

The number of amputees created by the disaster is hard to measure, but Handicap International estimates it is at least 2,000 and growing. Dr. Mitra Roses of the Pan American Health Organization said

51

some hospitals were performing between 30 and 100 amputations a day after the earthquake.
(articles.cnn.com/2010-01-27/world/haiti.amputees_1_amputees-haiti-international-limbs?_s=PM:WORLD)

Irwin Redlener, director for the National Center for Disaster Preparedness at the Columbia University Mailman School of Public Health, says the most immediate concerns will be severe head and chest injuries, but that doctors will also have to carefully manage all wounds, even small ones, to avoid infection and septic shock.... Any survivors pulled from the rubble in the next twenty-four hours are likely to be weaker than those rescued yesterday; they will be dehydrated, especially with temperatures in Port-au-Prince topping 90 degrees. If victims are also suffering from "crush injuries" after being struck or trapped under falling debris, they will be at risk of kidney failure—damaged muscles release proteins that are toxic to the organs—and in need of extra hydration to prevent it. "It's highly likely that we're going to see a lot of patients who survive this trauma and then have exacerbations of existing conditions like diabetes and asthma, or who develop stress-related medical disorders like coronary artery disease and hypertension." Mental health issues and post-traumatic stress disorder, which can set in any time in the six months or so after a disaster, will be "absolutely overwhelming."
(www.newsweek.com/2010/01/13/haiti-s-health-from-bad-to-worse.html)

The impact of the number of injuries and deaths is unimaginable in an era where there was no America or other wealthy country that could send teams of doctors, rescuers, water, and tons of medical supplies. The initial help came only from the few healthy survivors and the ambulating injured, who could make no impact on the situation. Only God was able to provide the resources for man's survival, and he did so through an outpouring of angels.

> Hebrews 12:22: But ye are come unto Mount Zion, and unto the city of the living God, the heavenly Jerusalem, and to an innumerable company of angels.

The angels arrived in large numbers and did whatever was necessary to prevent further injuries and deaths. They came with the knowledge and power of heaven to minister in desperate times. The scope of their actions evoked the well-known phrase that "desperate times require desperate measures."

> According to the *Oxford Dictionary of Quotations*, on the 6th November 1605, Guy Fawkes is reputed to have said, "The desperate disease requires a dangerous remedy" … which is very similar to "*extremis malis extrema remedia*" (Latin: "Extreme remedies for extreme ills"). (Thanks to Fred Shapiro, Yale Law Library)
> (wiki.answers.com/Q/Who_said_'Drastic_times_call_for_drastic_measures_'_and_when)

What were the extreme measures that had to be undertaken to save the people? When massive tectonic plates beneath the earth slide, there are severe consequences on the surface. The emerging countries were strewn with victims who needed medical care involving organ transplants, bone and tissue repair, and tissue replacements, but where were available organs for transplantation, the bones to replace crushed ones, and the flesh to repair the many wounds? There were no organized systems of medical care to meet the immense crisis; whatever was needed had to be gleaned from earth. The only available resources on earth were man, animals, plants, and possibly some primitive medical concoctions. Man was created as living tissue, so the only options were other forms of living tissue, either from man or animal. The acquisition of replacement parts is the key element behind some of the archaeological finds dating to the megalithic era. Archaeologists have found parts of pigs, sheep, and deer in excavated pits with human remains. There are wide speculations on the reason for the presence of these animal parts, because there has been no evidence found that they were consumed. It is possible that the items found in the pits are testimonies to the current research in xenotransplantation, in which certain animals fill the great demand for organ transplants in humans. There was surely a great demand after the earthquakes that split Pangaea.

> Xenotransplantation [is] defined as the transplantation of organs from other animal species into humans.... Research has focused in large part on pig organs and tissues because their biochemical profile is similar to that of human organs.... Current interest in xenotransplantation is fueled by promising results and significant demand. It addresses an acute shortage of organs for transplantation, but has a long way to go before it is an accepted and even routine clinical therapy.
> (www.nature.com/nbt/journal/v18/n10s/full/nbt1000_IT53.html)

> They conclude, "The potential benefits of successful xenotransplantation to large numbers of patients with very differing clinical conditions remain immense,

fully warranting the current efforts being made to work towards its clinical introduction."
(www.medicalnewstoday.com/articles/77365)

There must be some evidence of how mankind survived the great catastrophe of continental separation without the likes of modern medicine. The concept of xenotransplantation might be difficult for some people to comprehend, but considering the lack of alternative in such a deadly crisis, xenotransplantation was a dire necessity. The disaster caused multiple organ failures along with the need for numerous amputations. The angels worked swiftly and launched their healing program, which included xenotransplantation, because they understood that man was created from nature and is akin to all flesh, and all flesh belongs to God. Angels have the knowledge of creation and the relationships of man, animals, and nature and know the common denominators of all. They gleaned the necessary resources from the earth, which included collections of parts of animals and humans to complete their extreme measures for the extreme medical condition on the new continents created from the split of Pangaea.

The following paragraphs highlight the species of animals most commonly found by archaeologists and the clinical implications of each. The most dominant findings were bones of domestic pigs.

It is immediately apparent that pig dominated the assemblage and comprised almost 99 percent of the material. During the analysis of the pig bone, an attempt was made to identify any diagnostic characteristics of wild boar, but all the material was consistent with domestic pig. Of the 4,874 bone fragments identified as pig, 4,866 (99.8 percent) were fragments from the skull and teeth.

The volume and relative percentage of pig fragments recovered during these excavations make this assemblage stand out from others recovered from local sites of a similar date. In other words, a domestic assemblage usually displays more variation in species.

Third molars are common in the assemblage, but frequently only as tooth crowns. Those third molars which have fully erupted show either little or no wear. This would suggest that the pigs represented are younger (up to approximately two years) rather than older animals.

The involvement of pig skulls and the lack of evidence for butchery make feasting an unlikely explanation. (Chanctonbury Ring revisited, The Excavation of 1988-91, ads.ahds.ac.uk/catalogue/adsdata/arch-285-1/ahds/dissemination/pdf/vol_ 139/03_ rudling.pdf)

Currently, biological research is being conducted on the potential use of pigs to provide organ transplants in humans. Much of the research shows promise for the not-too-distant future. It is curious that the research involves very young and fetal pigs, which are the same age category as those found at the archaeological sites.

**Pigs**

All of the major structures found in humans are present in the fetal pig. With proper directions, they can all be readily found, especially with large, full-term fetal pig specimens.

In almost every case, fetal pigs have the same muscles as humans, with some small variations in the size and location of some muscles related to the fact that pigs are quadrupedal and humans are bipedal. For example, the major chest and abdominal muscles found in humans are present in the pig. There are some differences in the location of chest muscles that attach to the shoulder girdle. In the hind limb, the pig has the same muscles as humans in the major thigh muscle groups: quadriceps femoris and the hamstrings; in the hip, however, there are some differences in the gluteal muscles.
(www.goshen.edu/bio/PigBook/ humanpigcomparisonl)

CNN has been invited by one of South Korea's leading cloning experts, Dr. Hwang Woo-Suk, to witness a rare event in genetic science, the birth of "humanized" pigs. These genetically modified animals' organs have been tailor-made so that the size of them will allow them to be transplanted into humans.

Pig heart valves are widely used to patch up human hearts, but one of the biggest problems in using the entire organ is ensuring the human body doesn't reject it. Hwang has already successfully transplanted pig hearts into dogs. He told CNN that the same will be performed on monkeys later this year and projects that successful organ transplants from pigs to humans is not far off.
(www.cnn.com/2005/TECH/02/23/spark.pigs/ index.html)

Much like human teeth, the teeth of the pig have an

enamel coating, which makes the teeth of the pig stronger and less exposed to disease. Pigs are one of the few wild animals that properly chew their food as pigs have a digestive system that is similar to that of the human and therefore cannot digest unchewed food easily.
(a-z-animals.com/animals/pig)

As with humans, pigs feature molars, premolars (or bicuspids), canines, and incisors, and similar to most mammals, pigs and humans are diphyodont, or develop and erupt two generations of teeth into their jaws.
(www.olympusmicro.com/micd/galleries/darkfield/enamelformationpig)

There were also excavations of parts of sheep, deer, and ox. Each has a significant anatomical relationship to man. There are findings that consist of combinations of various animal parts with human bones that are typical throughout the megalith sites. Deer antlers have been almost as prominent as the bones of young pigs.

Heaps of antler picks were found in ditch terminal at Marden and Durrington.
(books.google.com/books?id=wj09AAAAIAAJ&pg=PA71&lpg=PA71&dq=red+deer+durrington+walls&source)

In the Long Barrow of West Kennet, too, were found numerous fragments of pottery, and with these fragments boars' tusks longer than those of the boar of the present clay, the bones of sheep, goats, roe deer, pigs, and of a large species of ox, all of which are probably relics of a funeral feast.

Quantities of antler picks have been taken from this much-abused conical hill whose steep sides indicate that it possesses a planned stability comparable with Sillsbury.
(www.stonehenge-avebury.net/aburysites.html)

The composition of deer antlers has a clear relationship to the development of human bones and tissue. Current products made from deer antlers have shown promise in healing and producing growth in human bones.

## Deer

Antler is a simple extension of bone … its composition is similar to that of human bones. Thus, one of the therapeutic roles of taking deer antler is as a source of calcium to help prevent or treat osteoporosis, which is consistent with the traditional bone-strengthening action of deer antler.

Scientists hope to one day understand the chemical mechanisms that spur the antler's growth. This could lead to a breakthrough in understanding how to regenerate tissue, or even how to re-create organs in humans.

Practitioners use velvet antler primarily to promote virility, replenish vital essence and blood, strengthen the bone and tendons, promote draining of abscesses, and regulate meridians (relative to the uterus and conception in women.)

Velvet antler is derived from several species of deer, but consists mainly of the young pilose (or hairy) antlers of two major deer species, Cervus nippon, the

Japanese or Asian deer (known as hua-lu-rong), and Cervus elaphus, the European red deer (ma-lu-rong). (The Herb Companion, www.herbcompanion.com/ herb-profiles/Velvet-antler.aspx

Velvet antler is a mainstay of traditional Chinese medicine, probably second only to ginseng in importance. Velvet antler does not refer to the velvety "skin" on growing antlers, but rather the whole cartilaginous antler in a precalcified stage. Typically the antler is cut off near the base after it is about two thirds of its potential full size, and before any significant calcification occurs.... The antler is dried and is used powdered or in tea form for a wide variety of health remedy and health maintenance purposes. Velvet antler is said to be effective as an anti-inflammatory, anticancer, immune stimulant, and progrowth agent. Western scientific studies have supported some of the claims, particularly the anti-inflammatory effects and athletic performance enhancement.
(en.wikipedia.org/wiki/Velvet_antler)

The sheep offers more than wool for clothing; parts such as the heart and eyes are identical to the human anatomy.

## Sheep

The sheep heart is very similar in size and shape to the human heart—slightly larger than the average human heart, but otherwise very similar.

The sheep eye is identical to the human eye in all major respects.

The sheep brain has the same basic plan as all

mammalian brains, including humans. Compared to a human brain, the sheep brain has a relatively smaller cerebral cortex and consequently a relatively smaller overall size. The other major parts are identical in terms of gross anatomy.
(www.goshen.edu/bio/PigBook/ humanpigcomparison)

Angels existed prior to creation and were part of the creation activities, which included the formation of man from the dust of the ground. They are privy to advance knowledge of the composition and functions of the human body. Scientists today have achieved great advancements in medical science and are gaining ground in eliminating the rejection of organ and tissue during transplantation. While man struggles to unlock the secret to transplantation, angels already possessed the knowledge and were able to negate incompatibilities. Thus, angels were able to perform the traumatic surgeries that men are now striving to achieve. The utilization of the parts of animals was part of the extreme measure taken by the angels to salvage mankind during the great disaster.

So then, angels are spirit beings with greater knowledge and power than human beings (2 Peter 2:11), created for the purpose of assisting those called and begotten by God.
(The Restored Church of God, www.thercg.org/ articles/agms.html)

Animals were possibly the most abundant resource but not the only source of organ and tissue donations. Many excavation sites have revealed various collections of human bones and full human skeletons that were laid out in very curious arrays. The strange arrangements seem to suggest that someone had plans for the bones which were in process or scheduled. A noted aftermath of earthquakes is the large number of bone injuries among the survivors; as was previous asked, where were there resources for bone repair and replacements? Two large and very questionable collections were found in the Sénégambian region of Africa, which dated to the megalithic era.

Sénégambian stone circles come in several forms.... Bones were placed here after the rest of the body decomposed at a primary site. The bones, usually from several bodies, were arranged according to an elaborate plan that no one today understands.

Holl told me about his excavations in the area: One turned up five full bodies, with all ten legs bent to form a pattern. In another circle, he and his team found twenty skulls on one side, and on the other, iron spearheads, and hundreds of thigh and arm bones (one still wearing a copper bracelet). Several of the circles have an upper layer of jawbones covered with upside-down clay pots.

The next day we went to Holl's dig at Santhiou Ngayène, where one circle grave was found to contain long bones lined up vertically in a circle, like a white picket fence. Inside the fence were more skulls, and closer to the surface, more pots and teeth.... After several hours, we had uncovered a group of skulls and long bones.
(Boston.com, In Africa, stone circles speak across the ages, www.boston.com/travel/getaways/africa/ articles/2008/09/28/in_africa_stone_circles_ speak_across_the_ages/?page=2)

The third enclosure [in Loanhead] is the first of several identical features that I have found round the

entire site. It is an almost circular area of bone and pottery mixed. This could either be just that—bones and shards of pot dumped in a pile. Or it could be a Cinerary Urn. As can be seen, I found seven of these objects in, or close to, the large ovals. There is also a larger area of bone and pottery in the southeastern quadrant—straddling the inner and outer face of the last oval. The area also contains a total of what appear to be five complete skeletons and three areas of bone without any real shape
(www.electricscotland.com/stones/loanhead.htm)

The pit [in Chanctonbury] contained early Iron Age pottery, animal and human bones, pieces of unworked dark red flint, the only pieces found on the site, and a piece of granite originating from Cornwall.
(www.steyningsouthdowns.com/places/chanctonbury_ring.asp)

Gray found few artifacts in the ditch fill [in Avebury] but did recover scattered human bones, jawbones being particularly well represented. At a depth of about 2 meters (7 feet), Gray encountered a complete skeleton of a woman 1.5 meters (5 feet) tall who had been buried there.
(www.crystalinks.com/avebury.html)

There was also a collection of human bones found at the Goseck Circle in Germany.

Nearby excavations of wood-and-clay houses have turned up a variety of grains and evidence of domesticated goats, sheep, pigs, and cows.... In addition to pottery shards and arrowheads within, excavators found the decapitated skulls of oxen, apparently displayed on poles, and parts of two human skeletons. The human bones were cleaned of flesh before being buried. Such ceremonies anoint the site as a temple, Bertemes notes, and show that science was inextricably entangled with superstition since Neolithic times.

(www.stonepages.com/news/archives/000475.html)

The various arrays of bones, especially the collection that is described as being like a "white picket fence," show preparations for surgery involving the replacement of damaged human bones among the survivors. The bones of the dead were not cremated if the living had need of them. There were no artificial prosthetics to replace crushed bones, and one common result of earthquakes is the many instances of injuries that led to amputations. Possibly, one team of angels collected parts from humans and animals throughout the region and the world, while others provided the trauma care. There were piles of animal and human bones because the angels moved swiftly until the completion of their mission. As with all medical procedures, it is better to have an abundance rather than a shortage of supplies.

In addition to the animal and human resources available for healing, there were also the findings of other medical resources such as shellfish, primarily oysters, which were found in some cases with collections of bones. The clinical implications of oysters to human healing have been outlined in modern biological research:

To the west of the main temple, a layer of rubble was found which covered another layer of oyster shells which lay on top of bare chalk bedrock.... Similar shell deposits have been discovered at other temples, such as at Hayling Island in nearby Hampshire.

(www.steyningsouthdowns.com/places/chanctonbury_ring.asp)

Oysters contain a compound called "nacre," which is an ideal substance for use with the treatment of various bone ailments.

Nacre, also known as mother of pearl, is an organic-inorganic composite material produced by some mollusks as an inner shell layer; it is also what makes up pearls. It is very strong, resilient, and iridescent.

A human bone heals, as does a cracked oyster's shell. We now believe nacre can be used to stimulate bone growth…. "More than 4,000 years ago, the Maya people of central America realized that nacre was not only beautiful but extremely hard and durable. They used it to make false teeth."

(www.independent.co.uk/life-style/health-and-families/health-news/healing-powers-of-oysters-could-mend-human-bones-395527.html)

This study demonstrates that nacre stimulates bone-forming cells in vertebrae and appears to result in new bone formation.

(ScienceDirect, Bone reactions to nacre injected percutaneously into the vertebrae of sheep, www.sciencedirect.com/science?_ob=ArticleURL&_udi=B6TWB-42397W16&_user=10&_coverDate=03%2F15%2F2001&_rdoc=1&_fmt=high&_orig=search&_sort=d&_docanchor=&view=c&_searchStrId=1225503202&_rerunOrigin=google&_acct=C000050221&_version=1&_urlVersion=0&_userid=10&md5=d9f26bf30928fd4f3096cd833906c89f)

An experiment using ground mother-of-pearl (nacre) from the bivalve mollusk Pinctada maxima, mixed with the blood of eight female patients suffering from bone loss in the upper jaw, has been undertaken. The mix was injected into tissues where bone was missing, and later biopsies showed no inflammatory reactions, and bone-forming cells had been activated, with new healthy bone forming. Although nacre and bone are not homologous as such, some of the complicated machinery driving their formation may be.
(www.faqs.org/abstracts/Zoology-and-wildlife-conservation/A-marriage-of-bone-and-nacre-Clinical-experiments-aimed-at-reducing-bone-loss-in-jaws-raise-a-raft-o.html)

But Mr. Milet's discovery is not going appear in the world's hospitals immediately. "We have already carried out in vivo bone graft tests in which we have obtained a perfect bond between the nacre and the bone. The medical uses of the biomineralization will be seen some years into the future," he said. "We have already asserted that not only can nacre be grafted on to bone and be accepted by the human body, it also releases active molecules which induce bone regeneration."
(Christian Milet is a biologist at the Museum National d'Histoire Naturelle in Paris)
(www.independent.co.uk/life-style/health-and-families/health-news/healing-powers-of-oysters-could-mend-human-bones-395527.html)

The angels used the nacre from the oysters to heal injured bones that didn't need replacement. They had the knowledge and the power to use the natural resources for the healing benefit of man.

The work of the angels lets us understand that even though man has the inner presence of a soul, his body is very much akin to all flesh. Prehistoric man was forced to bear this fact after scores of medical procedures were completed with the use of animal parts. They also saw the people, who would have normally been immediately consecrated to the ground after death, become donors to the survivors. The proud people from Shinar who wanted to make a name for themselves began to understand who they really were. They were created by God and belonged to God.

The common interpretation of all archaeological finds as part of sacrificial ceremonies and communal rituals has caused us to miss the messages in other areas of ancient studies, such as cave paintings. There is a particular cave drawing that I believe is related to the healing episodes by angels after the split of Pangaea. The painting is of a man with deer antlers (Figure 11). The painting has been interpreted as a representative of a masked medicine man, but I see a message that was difficult to relay in any other manner than a man with antlers. It is the only way prehistoric man could relay to the world that mankind was saved by the manipulation of the genetics of man and animals.

**Figure 11. Man with Antlers**
Source C is one of a number of prehistoric paintings that
show a man with antlers on his head, sometimes standing
in a circle with twelve other men. Some historians think
this shows a religious ritual, others that it might show
a medicine man. (www.pearsonschoolsandfecolleges.
co.uk/FEAndVocational/Humanities/History/
OCRGCSESchoolsHistoryProject/Samples/
OCRGCSEHistoryASchoolsHistoryProjectStudent
BookSamplePages/
GCSE%20OCR%20Schools%20History%20Project%20
-revised.pdf)

Further study of reports on cave paintings such as those found in the famous caves of Lascaux, France, reveal a strange obsession of the prehistoric man in drawing animals to the exclusion of humans, nature, village life, or celestial bodies. Animals were painted elaborately while humans were depicted as stick figures. The paintings were also drawn deep into caverns, far from the entrances and often in caverns that were not easily accessible.

> The painted walls of the interconnected series of caves in Lascaux in southwestern France are among the most impressive and well-known artistic creations of Paleolithic humans. Although there is one human image (painted representations of humans are very rare in Paleolithic art; sculpted human forms are more common), most of the paintings depict animals found in the surrounding landscape, such as horses, bison, mammoths, ibex, aurochs, deer, lions, bears, and wolves.... No vegetation or illustration of the environment is portrayed around the animals, who are represented in profile and often standing in an alert and energetic stance.... Most of the paintings are located at a distance from the cave's entrance, and many of the chambers are not easily accessible. This placement, together with the enormous size and compelling grandeur of the paintings, suggests that the remote chambers may have served as sacred or ceremonial meeting places.
>
> (www.metmuseum.org/toah/hd/lasc/hd_lasc.htm)

In striking contrast to the superbly rendered animals are the crude portrayals of the human form. With only a few known exceptions—important because they demonstrate that the cave artists were not simply incapable of drawing the human form accurately—the

men are depicted in the most rudimentary caricatures, their figures nothing more than scrawls comparable to the work of small children. One interpretation is that the realistic depiction of the human form was banned by a powerful religious taboo.
( w w w . e a r t h f a c t s . n e t / h u m a n s / cavepaintingsprehistoricartists/)

It is incredible that such vivid works of art are found in inaccessible and dangerous caves. It seems there was something occurring outside of the caves that required the artists to paint in secrecy in highly secluded areas. It also seems that the primary focus of whatever was taking place outside the caves involved animals. Animals had assumed a status greater than humans and nature. There was indeed something occurring outside the caverns that produced apprehension or even fear in the prehistoric artists. The animals were being used by the angels for the healing of mankind.

There is also a drawing of an excavation of a burial site that further highlights the message of xenotransplantation (Figure 12). The burial contained skeletal remains of a young girl with several racks of deer antlers and oyster shells. The many antler racks and the shells tell the story of someone's familiarity with the healing process; they knew some of the primary elements that were needed. It appears that the person wanted to facilitate the healing of bones by having the antlers and the shells readily available. The hope for healing in this case was obviously not fulfilled.

There was an excavation at Stonehenge that also highlights the people's familiarity with the healing process. The remains of a child were found with a chalk carving of a pig.

A carved animal figurine found buried alongside a prehistoric baby at Stonehenge may represent Britain's earliest known toy, researchers say.... The unique chalk relic of a hedgehog or pig, thought to be at least 2,000 years old, was unearthed in September near the stone monument on southern England's Salisbury Plain.

(n e w s . n a t i o n a l g e o g r a p h i c . c o m / news/2008/10/081021-stonehenge-toy.html)

Some archaeologists suggest that the carving of a pig on chalk was a toy put in the grave with the child as a sentimental gesture. I see instead someone's familiarity with the healing process and a plea for help. After many sick and injured people were healed, the people possibly began to realize what animals were beneficial for certain diseases. The Olmos Dam victim and the child victim were possibly part of actions taken after the angels had ceased the massive healing campaign and after the transporters were no longer present or making frequent visitations. The people possibly wanted to give the healers a hint of their diagnosis of the victims' problems in the event the healers returned.

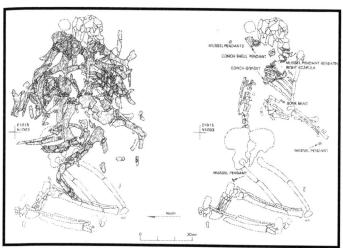

**Figure 12. Skeletal Remains Found at Olmos Dam**
www.texasbeyondhistory.net/st-plains/images/ap10.html

(Olmos Dam, Texas) Drawing of the burial of a young woman (sixteen to nineteen years old) at the Olmos Dam site near the headwaters of the San Antonio River. Her body was covered with nine white-tail deer antler racks (and attached skull fragments), which were a common grave offering at this cemetery. Beneath the antlers, in the vicinity of her neck, wrists, and ankles, were freshwater and marine shell ornaments and a bone bead.

Some of the archaeological sites have residual evidence of medical processes similar to modern-day medical practice. For instance, modern operating rooms include necessary hardware such as tables, lamps, chairs, cabinets, and respiratory, suction, and drainage systems. These are all constructed with the metals and coverings characteristic of this era. But what would the equipment look like if the same medical procedures were performed thousands of years BC when aluminum, plastic, rubber, and refined cloth were not yet available? The only materials available at that time for construction were the ground, stones, timber, and fur of animals. So an operating table could look like a large grooved stone slab with a crude drainage system nearby, such as can be found at the megalithic site of Mystery Hill, Vermont (Figure 13).

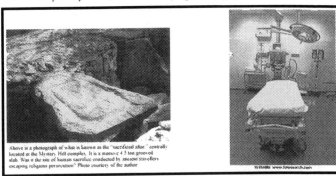

Above is a photograph of what is known as the "sacrificial altar" centrally located at the Mystery Hill complex. It is a massive 4.5 ton grooved slab. Was it the site of human sacrifice conducted by ancient travellers escaping religious persecution? Photo courtesy of the author

**Figure 13. Mystery Hill Stone Slab**

The notation below the above picture of the huge stone slab states:

> Above is a photograph of what is known as the "sacrificial altar," centrally located at the Mystery Hill complex. It is a massive 4x5 ton grooved slab. Was it the site of human sacrifice conducted by ancient travelers escaping religious persecution?

> One of the central features of the Mystery Hill site is the sacrificial table/altar. It is a 4.5 ton grooved slab whose purpose is still under debate by scholars. In the words of archeologist and Mystery Hill curator Robert Stone, "Others believe it was used for sacrifices, not only because of its central location, its size, but also because the Oracle speaking tube was beneath it, as well as the carved channel [for the draining of blood] on the top surface. It is positioned on four worked stone legs and is located at the center of the site in a large courtyard."
> (planetvermont.com/pvq/v9n1/megaliths.html)

Medical care was given in the transporters, on stone slabs, in the fields, and in the spaces with the stone furniture that were once part of the structures in the Plains of Shinar.

The physical healing of man was the primary goal, but just as in modern times, physical healing needed to be accompanied by mental well-being. The angels had to help men accept what had happened to them and guide them through periods of adjustments. There is a controversial and very peculiar medical procedure that originated in ancient times and continues today. The procedure, called "trepanation," was practiced and intended to promote mental well-being as part of the holistic approach to medical care.

# Chapter 7: Trepanation

As the people began to look around and truly realized the extent of the healings, they saw an increase in living activities, and many gained hope that God would spare them and their land. But for others, the tragedy of Pangaea left permanent mental trauma that is often common with disaster victims. The angels came as healers, but their strange presence might have also contributed to the mental stress of the moment. In the Bible, many people were bewildered, frightened, and almost in shock at the presence of the angels. In an effort to treat mental depression, it is possible that the angels introduced to man an extreme measure for extreme mental illness called "trepanation." This procedure, whose origin baffles modern scientists, is performed to induce a better state of mind.

> Trepanation is the practice of making a hole in the skull in order to improve the brain pulsations and hence the overall well-being.... The idea is to pump up the brain blood volume. It's known that one's level of consciousness is directly related to the volume of blood in one's brain. As a result, trepanners say, one feels happier and more energetic. The practice of trepanation has been around since the Stone Age. (www.trepanationguide.com/)

Trepanation is one of the oldest surgical procedures

being practiced by humans. Skulls with holes bored in them have been found by archaeologists from as far back as 3000 BC. The oldest of these occur in the Danube Basin. Hundreds of skulls with traces of trepanation are known all over Europe—in Denmark, Sweden, Poland, France, Spain, and the British Isles. (www.trepanationguide.com/history.htm)

According to the International Trepanation Advocacy Group, the blood flow enhancement attained by skull trepanation resembles the blood flow characteristics of youth, and on this basis, the reduced blood flow through the brain characteristic of middle age can be restored to a youthful level.
(www.trepan.com/)

I don't believe that ancient man discovered that a hole in the head would regulate the blood volume level in the brain and produce a better feeling of consciousness. If the procedure was performed by ancient men, I believe the ability to perform such a procedure came from eyewitness accounts and perhaps even instructions from the angels. If hundreds of skulls with holes were found in Europe, it seems trepanation flourished in those areas for a period of time. Those are the areas where we find the majority of megalith monuments.

It was imperative that the people gain enough motivation to move on to face the future, or all hopes would have been destroyed at the Tower of Babel. The people had sacrificed their individual dreams for the common goal of building the tower. After the catastrophes, they were challenged to develop new lives with their new languages in new lands and with the understanding that they had rebelled against God.

There was one other mental challenge that the people eventually realized over a period of time, that was part of the plan to separate them for the purpose of filling the earth. They realized there were changes occurring in their physical features, and those changes were altering their visual perception of oneness. They were gradually becoming dissimilar to each other in physical appearance.

# Chapter 8:   Changes in
# Physical Appearance

There is much debate on how the differences in the physical characteristics of men occurred if the world was repopulated by Noah's family after the Flood. Those debates have centered on possible genetic mutations over centuries and the possible effect of the environment on the production of melanin in the body, which controls skin pigmentation. If the world was repopulated by Noah's family, it seems that the complexion of the population would have developed in similar fashions throughout the world. The families of Noah were as all families, in that the members resembled one another in complexion and facial features. In each generation, there are the physical reminders of the relationship with the parent generation. Regardless of the different scientific debates, I believe the overall factor to be considered is the will of God. It was God's intention to destroy the unity at the Tower of Babel and cause a great dispersing of the population to fill the earth. Were the confusion of the languages and the split of Pangaea sufficient to accomplish this? I believe the angels manipulated the chemistry of man to cause the development over time of the different physical characteristics between "races." Those differences have proven even in modern times to be a great separator of men. This is evident in the regional populations of Asians, Europeans, Africans, Native

Americans, and South Americans. Consider the thought that when men began to sail and travel to other continents, they did not find men who resembled them; they did not readily acknowledge any relationship to the foreigners and were not willing to assimilate their culture into theirs or vice versa. I believe similarity in physical traits was one of the main reasons the people of Shinar were able to maintain their strong cohesion. The eventual development of the differences in the physical traits and the new languages and the new continents forced man to spread permanently across the globe.

The angels knew earth's geography and understood that men who were dispersed to certain region of the world would need more melanin in their bodies than others. If the amount of melanin was not adjusted for those who were dispersed to an area like Africa, they would have survived the split of Pangaea only to eventually die of overexposure to the sun.

> Melanin: A skin pigment (substance that gives the skin its color). Dark-skinned people have more melanin than light-skinned people. Melanin also acts as a sunscreen and protects the skin from ultraviolet light.
> (www.medterms.com/script/main/art.asp?articlekey=4340)

> Melanin (protein): Pigments largely of animal origin. High molecular weight polymers of indole quinone. Colors include black/brown, yellow, red, and violet. Found in feathers, cuttle ink, human skin, hair, and eyes, and in cellular immune responses and wound healing in arthropods.
> (www.biology-online.org/dictionary/Melanin)

It is curious that melanin is "largely of animal origin," as stated by scientists. As previously stated in this book, the resources the angels used to accomplish their mission were gleaned from the earth. The animals provided resources for healing through xenotransplantation and also provided the product for activating the final phase of separation. The melanin changes and the manipulation of other genetic factors completed the final phase of separation through changes in the physical characteristics of man.

The people did not know that as they were forced to other lands, physiological changes would occur over time and make them appear to be unrelated. Some scientists believe in the randomness of nature in producing various forms of life and have somewhat applied the concept of randomness to man. I believe the changes in man were governed by the will of God. The debate over genetics will continue far into the future, but the will of God is known and expressed in the Scriptures. The inability of scientists to pinpoint how the descendants of Noah became so diverse early in the history of mankind is due to the fact that the mutations were products of superior intelligence and God's desire for the whole world to be teeming, as it is today.

# Chapter 9:    Strange
# Fires upon Stones

The angels were competent, efficient, and resourceful in their healing campaign, and there were operational logistics to be managed, such as how to transport in and out of the regions and how to minimizing their daily contacts with humans. The angels needed to be able to move around the world from region to region without having to travel across vast areas of land. So, they used the chariots of fire to deliver them individually or in groups to various regions of the world and were picked up after the missions were completed. The idea has been commonly accepted that angels have wings with which they fly to earth and beyond. However, there are scriptural references in the Bible that seems to raise questions as to the angels' mode of transportation. For instance, there are the stories of Elijah and the chariot of fire and the altar of Manoah upon which there was a flame of fire. Even though John saw angels fly in heaven, there seem to be restrictions upon them in their assumption of human forms on earth. These restrictions have required angels to take certain measures that I believe are reflected in the ancient burnt stones and burnt mounds at many megalithic sites. These stones and mounds show the method and places the angels used to arrive at and depart from regions around the earth. We get a glimpse of the restrictions and the mode of transportation when we review the biblical story of Manoah and his wife's encounter with an angel.

> Judges 13:19–20: So Manoah took a kid with a meal offering, and offered it upon a rock unto the Lord; and the angel did wondrously, and Manoah and his wife looked on. For it came to pass, when the flame went up toward heaven from off the altar, that the angel of the Lord ascended in the flame of the altar. And Manoah and his wife looked on and fell on their faces to the ground.

The story of Manoah and the angel gives us a different perspective on the use of fires upon stone slabs. Manoah began a fire for the burning of a sacrifice, and the angel performed some actions with the fire that drastically altered the nature of the flames. I believe the angel transformed the flame into a method of communication to notify a chariot of fire of his location and need for transport. The Scripture says, "For it came to pass," which implies a waiting period and later a flamelike phenomenon was provided for the angel. Without delving too deeply into physics, I would like to note that the composition of a natural flame involves plasma and infrared light. Both plasma and infrared light can be used for signaling through space.

> A flame is an exothermic, self-sustaining, oxidizing chemical reaction producing energy and glowing hot matter, of which a very small portion is plasma. It consists of reacting gases and solids emitting visible and infrared light, the frequency spectrum of which depends on the chemical composition of the burning elements and intermediate reaction products. (www.answerbag.com/q_view/592642)

Like gas, plasma does not have a definite shape or a definite volume unless enclosed in a container; unlike gas, under the influence of a magnetic field, it may form structures such as filaments, beams, and double layers. Some common plasmas are stars and neon signs.
(en.wikipedia.org/wiki/Plasma_(physics)

We know that infrared radiation is light just like visible light because it has the same properties as visible light. Infrared can be focused and reflected like visible light. Infrared light can also be "aligned" like regular light and therefore polarized. This means we can make infrared telescopes that look and work the way normal visible light telescopes do.
astro.uchicago.edu/cara/about_cara/defn/irlight.html

It is possible that the advanced knowledge of the angel gave him the ability to transform the flame on the altar into a communication medium by which he was able to receive assistance in leaving the area. I consider the actions of the angels to be similar to today's wireless communication which, like the flame of a fire, involves a common element of infrared light.

Wireless operations permits services, such as long-range communications, that are impossible or impractical to implement with the use of wires. The term is commonly used in the telecommunications industry to refer to telecommunications systems (e.g., radio transmitters and receivers, remote controls, computer networks, network terminals, etc.) which use some form of energy (e.g., radio frequency, infrared light, laser light, visible light, acoustic energy,

etc.) to transfer information without the use of wires. Information is transferred in this manner over both short and long distances.
(en.wikipedia.org/wiki/Wireless)

If we note the Scripture that states when the flame (singular) appeared to go up toward heaven from off the altar, we understand that the angel's actions were the cause of the appearance of the flamelike phenomenon. Common knowledge of fires helps us to understand that the material on the altar was not capable of producing a natural flame that extended high into the sky. A regular fire reaching that height would require much more flammable material such as would be found in a lumber yard or chemical plant fire. The "flame" was evidently very controlled because a natural fire with a flame reaching to the sky would have covered a large area of land. The Scriptures imply that there was one steady flamelike phenomenon that extended upward from the rock Manoah had prepared. The angel who was physically in the presence of Manoah ascended in the flamelike phenomenon. His actions in my opinion are a testament to Einstein's theory of relativity, which involves mass and energy conversion: $E = mc^2$.

## $E = mc^2$

The concept of mass–energy equivalence unites the concepts of conservation of mass and conservation of energy, allowing particles which have rest mass to be converted to other forms of energy which have the same mass but require motion, such as kinetic energy, heat, or light. Kinetic energy or light can also be converted to particles which have mass. The total mass inside an isolated (totally closed) system remains constant over time for any single observer in an inertial frame, because energy cannot be created or destroyed and, in all of its forms, trapped energy

has mass. According to the theory of relativity, mass and energy as commonly understood are two names for the same thing, and one is not changed to the other. Rather, neither one appears without the other. Thus, when energy changes type and leaves a system, it takes its mass with it.
(en.wikipedia.org/wiki/Mass%E2%80%93energy_equivalence)

The angel at Manoah's house approached the flamelike energy source and infused his body for transport away from the area. The mass that represented the angel was converted to conform with the energy of the flamelike phenomenon that extended downward to Manoah's altar. The angel was transported upward. When I review the concept of angels having wings to fly, I wonder why the angel at Manoah's house didn't simply fly away. His failure to do so seems to support the idea of mass/energy conversion and displacement on earth as compared to John's vision in the Bible of angels flying in heaven. I wonder if he could have also transported Manoah and his wife in the same manner. That thought evokes the question of whether some of the injured from the fall of Babel and the split of Pangaea were transported across the world to the primary staging areas of the United Kingdom, where so many ancient stone circles and other megalithic monuments are located. This fact would be of greater importance for areas of need that were not suitable for the landing of the transporter. It would also imply that angels were easily transported to remote areas by way of the flamelike phenomenon. The angel at Manoah's house received help the same way Elijah was transported upward to the "chariot of fire" and the same way the angels that Jacob saw were transported upward and downward upon a "ladder." This is the same type of flamelike phenomenon that delivered the angel to Moses at the burning bush in the Book of Exodus.

Exodus 3:2, 8: And the angel of the Lord appeared unto him in a flame of fire out of the midst of a bush; and he looked, and, behold the bush burned with fire, and the bush was not consumed.... "And I am come down to deliver them out of the land of the Egyptians."

An angel emerged from the flame of the burning bush to speak with Moses after arriving in the flame as indicated by his statement, "I am come down." So, we have an angel departing in a flame in the Book of Judges and an angel arriving in a flame in the Book of Exodus. I believe the angel that spoke with Moses also departed in the flamelike phenomenon of the bush. In the story with Moses, there was no prior fire upon stone before the angel's arrival, because the angel arrived on a mission for that moment and at that particular place. There was no need for any prior communications through fire upon stones.

I believe the transformation of fire upon stones was the manner of communication that was used by the angels at Stonehenge, Gungywamp, the burnt mounds called "fulachta fiadh" (Figure 14), and other megalithic sites. The burnt stones and the burnt mounds, like Manoah's altar, relay another facet of the angels' mission to save mankind and add another piece to the puzzle of the megaliths. This information is like more evidence of a crime with multiple crime scenes. I refer to one of the previous chapters on trauma care through xenotransplantation and human organ donations. The advanced trauma care required a gathering of animal and human parts in order to perform the necessary operations to save the injured and dying victims of the disaster of Pangaea. The healing campaign could possibly have involved human and animal parts delivery to various regions of the world or to the central location of the United Kingdom, or delivered to the United Kingdom to save those surrounded by freezing water.

Besides containing beehive chambers and petroglyphs, the Gungywamp site [Groton, Connecticut] has a double circle of stones near its center, just north of two stone chambers. Two concentric circles of large quarried stones—twenty-one large slabs laid end to end— are at the center of the site. Extensive fire burning on some of the slabs is apparent, which leads many to believe it was an ancient altar.

Burnt mounds are prehistoric monuments found throughout Britain and Ireland, Scandinavia, and parts of continental Europe.
www.shorewatch.co.uk/cruester/mounds.html

Around 1,600 burnt mounds, comprising heaps of fire cracked stones, up to several meters across with characteristic forms, are listed in the National Monuments Records of Scotland, with a diverse distribution. Many more are known in other parts of Europe, notably in Ireland and Scandinavia. (www.sciencedirect.com/burnt mounds)

Over thirty burnt mounds have been found in Birmingham. These are low mounds, usually 10 to 15 meters across, composed of heat-shattered stone, charcoal, and ash. Some of Birmingham's burnt mounds have been dated to between 1500 and 1000 BC by radiocarbon dating of the charcoal.

The most straightforward explanation of the usage of burnt mounds has always been that they were some form of seasonal cooking site, probably associated with hunting parties. At Watermead, as with the majority of excavated burnt mounds, there was an almost complete absence of cooking "debris" to support this.

(www.le.ac.uk/ulas/downloads/Burnt_Mounds.pdf)

The morphology of fulachta fiadh (plural) is very common in Ireland. A fulachta fian usually consists of a rectangular water trough that is lined either with slabs of stone or wood, and there are generally hearths nearby. Near the trough you would commonly find a pile of stones in a horse-shoe shape that have been burnt and cracked by heat.... The sites are usually located near water, and sometimes the remains of a wooden hut are found nearby.... Fulachta fiadh have been recorded in every county of Ireland.... There are an incredible 2,500 in County Cork.... The majority of dates range from a period beginning at c. 1400 BC and range to the early medieval period in Ireland, meaning that fulachta fiadh are a Bronze Age innovation.... We do not know conclusively what purpose they served or why so many were built.
www.angelfire.com/fl/burntmounds/whatarethey.html

The Gungywamp site has twenty-one stone slabs that show extensive fire burning. When I consider the host of angels that Jacob saw, I wonder how the host of angels transported in and out of the land. One altar or one burning bush with one flamelike phenomenon was sufficient for the transport of one angel, but it is possible that several angels or a small group needed an extensive arrangement involving several flamelike phenomena. Also, the complex at the Gungywamp site might indicate a place of regular arrival and departures due to the extensive amount of fire burning.

Another archaeological mystery that might also indicate

areas of frequent arrivals and departures are the many fulachta fiadh or burnt mounds found in the United Kingdom. Archaeologists are puzzled by the burnt stones in a horseshoe shape near water and no evidence of cooking. I believe the burnt mounds with their timber-formed wooden troughs show areas of frequent arrivals and departures and are the healing pools in the remote areas that served the same purpose as the Pool of Bethesda in the Bible.

**Figure 14.  Burnt Mounds**
Fulachta Fiadh
The burnt mounds at Liddle, South Ronaldsey, Orkney

With so many injured people scattered throughout the world, the angels who created the burnt mounds were mobilized in teams to certain areas for the purpose of healing all manner of injuries and diseases. They transported into the areas via the flamelike phenomenon from the chariots of fire and later signaled for pickup with the fires upon the stones.

*Angel picked up at Manoah's House*

*Bible*

*Elijah picked up in the midst of a whirlwind*

*Bible*

*Angels picked up at Jacob's Ladder*

*Bible*

*Angels picked up at Gungywamp*

*Megalithic Site*

**Figure 15 –Chariots of Fire Pickups in the Bible and at a Megalithic Site**

# Chapter 10: Biblical Reflections of Ancient Healings

Healings by the angels occurred on a massive scale to save the people after the split of Pangaea and continued on a much smaller scale as recorded in biblical history. There are two healing events in the Bible that mirror some of the circumstances of ancient healings and that give more information on healing activities at Stonehenge and other megalithic sites. Those two events are the healing of the paralytic man at the Pool of Bethesda and the healing of the blind man in the Pool of Siloam. All divine healings are related whether there is one person being heal or a multitude, because they are done by the same spirit and the same knowledge base. The event involving the paralytic man truly raises questions and seems to reflect ancient times.

> John 5:2–9: Now there is at Jerusalem, by the sheep gate, a pool, which is called in the Hebrew tongue Bethesda, having five porches. In these lay a great multitude of impotent folk, of blind, lame, paralyzed, waiting for the moving of the water. For an angel went down at a certain season into the pool, and troubled the water: whosoever then first, after the troubling of the water, stepped in was made well of whatever disease he had. And a certain man was there, who

had an infirmity thirty and eight years. When Jesus saw him lying there, and knew that he had been thus now a long time, he said unto him, Wilt thou be made well? The impotent man answered him, Sir, I have no man, when the water is troubled, to put me into the pool; but while I am coming, another steppeth down before me. Jesus saith unto him, Rise, take up thy bed, and walk. And immediately the man was made well, and took up his bed, and walked; and the same day was the Sabbath.

This Bible passage indicates that it was common knowledge that angels came to heal men at certain places on a seasonal basis. It is evident from the story of the Pool of Bethesda that mankind needed a continuous dose of angelic healing. Disease, disasters, and war constantly threatened the birth and death ratio, and man had not developed the sciences of today's modern medicine. Jesus went to the pool of Bethesda because he knew what the angels knew. He knew that as he drew the multitudes away from the pools to himself, there was one who was physically and perhaps mentally confined to the porch. The healing that the angel would have performed for the man was done by Jesus.

The story of this paralytic man raises a question as to why he was not healed in the pool. The paralytic man indicated that he would start and someone would get there before him. If he really wanted to be healed and he was fully aware that he could not move fast, why did he remain so far away from the pool? It seems that a better plan would have been to lay his bed by the pool's edge, and as soon as the water was stirred, he could then simply roll over or stretch out his hands into the pool. His failure to do so raises the question as whether he was acting on his own volition or according to certain instructions. It doesn't seem logical that the man would choose to return to the porch unless there was a requirement for him to do so or some type of hazard in remaining close to the pool. His actions bring to mind the perimeters at Stonehenge, the Ring of Brogar, the Goseck Circle, and other sites. It is possible that the immediate areas around the healing episodes were entered by invitations only and the people entered through restricted and designated entrances. The paralytic man stated that one would enter before him at the exclusion of another. It is inconceivable that an open healing pool with the sick lying around would not have many people entering simultaneously. This story brings to mind the difference between an open community pool and a baptismal pool at a church. The people are free to dive in at the open community pool but enter the baptismal pool only upon invitation by the minister, who is normally standing in the water. I believe the angels at Bethesda performed in an orderly manner just as the angels at the megalithic sites of ancient times. I don't believe the sick people were forced to struggle against each other to be healed. The injured and the dying were escorted into the waters at the River Avon near Stonehenge, the pools at the burnt mounds (Fulachta Fiadh), and the Pool of Bethesda.

The healing by the angel at Bethesda occurred during the time of official record keeping, yet there is nothing recorded but the stirring of the water. The same lack of records holds true for the stone circles and the burnt mounds. There is evidence of people but no record of their interactions with the healers. When the Bible speaks of Jesus healing someone, there is the presence of Jesus, the conversation between Jesus and the sick person, and the reaction of the healed person. But for the healings by the angels, there are no descriptions of the angels or any record of the interactions between the angels and the persons being healed. There seems to be an effort to maintain anonymity, or perhaps the people were not allowed to see what was taking place. However, they knew who the healers were. But how did they know, and who was the first to discover the healing opportunity at the Pool of

Bethesda? Since there are no detailed descriptions, there is the possibility that the knowledge of the healing at the pool was passed through generations as common knowledge as a result of previous healings. The many remains at Stonehenge seem to indicate that the people continued to go there based on a common knowledge of previous events of healings.

The second event in the Bible that reflects on the ancient healings at the megalithic sites is the story of the man who was born blind and the Pool of Siloam. After the fall of Babel and the split of Pangaea, there were numerous types of physical injuries due to the earthquakes, volcanoes, fire across the land, and rising and freezing waters. The repairs of the human body required bones and flesh. Xenotransplantation was one option for certain injuries, and another option was a miracle. This option involved the same elements that Jesus used during his healing of the man who was born blind.

> John 9:1, 6–7: And as Jesus passed by, he saw a man who was blind from his birth.... When he had thus spoken, he spat on the ground, and made clay of the spittle, and anointed the eyes of the blind with the clay. And he said unto him, "Go wash in the pool of Siloam" (which is by interpretation, Sent). He went his way, therefore, and washed, and came seeing.

> John 9:32: Since the world began was it not heard that any man opened the eyes of one that was born blind?

The above Scripture is very important, not only to show Jesus as the Creator but also to explain one aspect of the ancient healing events. John 9:32 gives the understanding that there was something different about this blind man in comparison with all other blind men in the Bible. This man was born with a genetic defect and did not have the mechanisms for sight.

The other blind men had the mechanisms for sight but they were malfunctioning. In those cases, Jesus touched them and was able to immediately correct the defect to give the men sight.

> Matthew 20:34: And Jesus had compassion on them, and touched their eyes, and immediately their eyes received sight, and they followed him.

However, in John 9:32, the mechanisms for sight were absent and had to be created as indicated by the phrase "opened the eyes of one that was born blind." The medical condition that the man had is today called "anophthalmia" or "microphthalmia."

> Anophthalmia and microphthalmia are often used interchangeably. Microphthalmia is a disorder in which one or both eyes are abnormally small, while anophthalmia is the absence of one or both eyes. These rare disorders develop during pregnancy and can be associated with other birth defects. (www.nei.nih.gov/health/anoph/anophthalmia. asp#a)

The actions that Jesus took to heal this particular blind man reveal a possible option that was available to the angels during the ancient healing events. Jesus took dirt from the ground, as God did during creation, and interjected a divine catalyst in his spittle and spirit and sent the man to the waters. The spirit then used the dirt from the ground and water to form the mechanisms for sight. The dirt and water became living tissue designed by Jesus, just as the dirt of the first man, Adam, became a living creature. In the ancient United Kingdom and elsewhere after the split of Pangaea, there were victims who needed organ and bone replacements, and there were others impaired due to genetic or hereditary defects. I believe the angels took a holistic approach to healing because a man who needed bone replacement but was born with a crippling genetic defect would still face a potentially early death. The angels' mission was to save as many lives as possible and to restore the people's ability to subdue the earth. Jesus' actions in the New Testament reveal the knowledge and the power of the spirit that was available to the angels during the ancient disaster, and the magnitude and the urgency of the catastrophe required the use of all available options. The story of the healing at the Pool of Bethesda confirms that angels did come to provide healing for man, and we can assume that the healings were performed at the waters such as the pools of the burnt mounds, the Pool of Bethesda, and the Pool of Siloam, and at the rivers such as the River Avon near Stonehenge.

> Stonehenge Avenue is an ancient avenue marked as a UNESCO World Heritage Site. Discovered in the eighteenth century, it measures nearly 3 kilometers, connecting Stonehenge with the River Avon. It was built during the Stonehenge 3 period of 2600 to 1700 BCE.
> (en.wikipedia.org/wiki/Stonehenge_Avenue)

> Excavations by the Stonehenge Riverside Project in 2005 discovered a monumental avenue linking Durrington Walls henge to the river.
> (ucl.ac.uk/prehistoric/past/past52/past52.html)

Healing of genetics defects in water was also displayed in a healing episode in the Old Testament involving Elisha and Naaman, the captain of the Syrian army, who was healed in the Jordan River.

> 2 Kings 5:9–10, 14: So Naaman came with his horses

and with his chariot, and stood at the door of the house of Elisha. And Elisha sent a messenger unto him, saying, Go and wash in the Jordan seven times, and thy flesh shall come again to thee, and thou shalt be clean.... Then went he down, and dipped himself seven times in the Jordan, according to the saying of the man of God; and his flesh came again like unto the flesh of a little child, and he was clean.

After studying the healings in the Bible, it is no surprise that Stonehenge and the Durrington Walls were connected to the River Avon, the burnt mounds were connected to pools of water, the many stone circles of Sénégambia, Africa, where large collections of human bones were found, lie along the River Gambia, and the vast majority of megalith sites in the United Kingdom lie along the coastal regions.

On 21 July 2006, the stone circles were added to the World Heritage List. They are described by UNESCO as consisting of four large groups of stone circles that represent an extraordinary concentration of over 1,000 monuments in a band 100 kilometers wide along some 350 kilometers of the River Gambia.

The presence of water is a common factor in both the ancient healings of the megalithic period and the events of healings in the Bible.

# Chapter 11:  Memorializing the Moment

After the people of the world fully realized the magnitude of what had occurred, they had to decide the best way to describe their experiences and display their gratitude. They saw the arrival of the chariots of fire; they felt the healing touches that mended their bodies and stopped their pains; they heard the screams and groan cease; and later, they heard their shouts of praises to God. They knew that the crushed bones were mended or replaced, and the vision that was taken away by a fall or a tumbling stone was restored. They also remembered the many dead and the fires for cremations. After periods of healing, the people decided on a definite way to show current and future generations what God had done to preserve mankind. The people who had labored together as one to build a tower in defiance of God joined together once again to accomplish a great task of building monuments in praise of him and his ministering angels.

Stonehenge is a monument that represents how the angels arrived, and the Carnac Stones (Figure 10) represent how the angels disembarked from their chariots of fire.

Carnac and its neighboring villages still hold in the region of 4,000 megalithic stones. Archaeologists

believe that the original amount was probably close to 10,000 stones.
(www.philipcoppens.com/carnac.html)

One factor that influences my belief that the Carnac Stones represent a procession of angels is the archaeological report that the original number of stones at the site was ten thousand. In the Bible the number ten thousands is used more than once to describe a company of angels:

> Jude 1:14–15: And Enoch also, the seventh from Adam, prophesied of these, saying, "Behold, the Lord cometh with ten thousands of his saints, to execute judgment upon all."

> Revelation 5:11: And I beheld, and I heard the voice of many angels round about the throne and the living creatures, and the elders, and the number of them was ten thousand times ten thousand, and thousands of thousands.

It seems that the creators of the Carnac Stones used a number of stones that would have meaning to Bible scholars with hope that the correlation between the monuments and angels would eventually be made. The display was obviously created to raise questions and to hopefully last until those questions could be answered. The Carnac Stones and other displays are indeed mysteries, but should we really be surprised that the stone monuments make references to experiences with God? After studying the biblical story about the crossing of the Jordan River by the Israelites under the leadership of Joshua, the question could be raised as to whether the stone monuments of ancient times were created voluntarily or per instructions.

Joshua 4:1–8: And it came to pass, when all the
people were completely passed over the Jordan,
that the Lord spoke unto Joshua, saying, "Take ye
twelve men out of the people, out of every tribe a
man, and command ye them, saying, 'Take here out
of the midst of the Jordan, out of the place where
the priests' feet stood firm, twelve stones, and ye
shall carry them over with you, and leave them in the
lodging place, where ye shall lodge this night.'" Then
Joshua called the twelve men, whom he had prepared
of the children of Israel, out of every tribe a man.
And Joshua said unto them, "Pass over before the ark
of the Lord your God into the midst of the Jordan,
and take ye up every man of you a stone upon his
shoulder, according unto the number of the tribes of
the children of Israel; That this may be a sign among
you, that when your children ask their fathers in time
to come, saying, 'What mean ye these stones?'"

The Book of Joshua chapter 4 shows that Joshua had
selected twelve exceptionally strong men who could carry large
stones upon their shoulders. The stones were large enough to
avoid being washed away or covered by the sands of time,
because the Scriptures state, "when your children ask their
fathers in time to come," which indicates that they should
survive the passing of time. The stones were also placed in
formation because the Scriptures also state that a stone was
taken to each tribe's "lodging place." When the Israelites
rested in the desert, they rested in formation according to
the commands of God (Figure 15). If each tribe left a stone
at the place of their lodging, the stones formed an outline of
the camp. The formation of the stones was the impetus for
the question, "What mean ye these stones?" A random display
of stones would not have produced much curiosity, due to

the fact that the Jordan River often overflowed its banks and could potentially wash stones ashore.

Joshua 3:15: For the Jordan overfloweth all its banks all the time of the harvest.

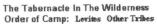

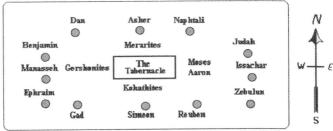

**Figure 16a. The Wilderness Tabernacle**
**(Dots inserted by the author to represents stones from the Jordan River) (Daily Bible Study, The Camp, www.keyway. ca/htm2000/20001016.htm)**

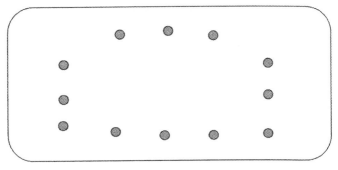

**Figure 16b. The Vacated Camp**
**The stones that were left in place when the tribes of Israel departed the area (Drawing by the author)**

Twelve smooth stones were chosen to commemorate the crossing of the Jordan River on dry ground. How many stones were appropriate to commemorate the saving of mankind by legions of angels? The stone circles and other megaliths are like the twelve stones in their purpose to evoke the question from the future generations of "What mean ye these stones?" The creators of the stone monuments chose a universal language in stone during a time after the languages had been confused at the Tower of Babel. The monuments were symbols that each in his language could relate to and remember the miraculous healings by angels.

There is much speculation as to how the people of ancient times carried the massive stones of Stonehenge and other sites across the land to their present location. Some speculate that the stones were floated down the river, and others believe that the stones were carried across frozen land or ice. Researchers are also baffled by early man's ability to move massive stones to a position around a circle. They have found evidence of the presence of people but no evidence of the technology to transport stones that weigh forty tons. Even today, a motorized vehicle is usually required to move stones weighing forty tons. Transport upon ice offers a plausible idea; however, I believe that the people who built Stonehenge are some of the remnants of the people of the Plain of Shinar who were trapped in the area of the United Kingdom following the split of Pangaea. They were very familiar with the process of brick making that was used at the Tower of Babel. The immense size of the tower probably required just about everyone to be skilled in the art of brick making and hoisting.

> Genesis 11:3: And they said one to another, "Come, let us make brick, and burn them thoroughly." And they had brick for stone, and slime had they for mortar.

I believe the Tower of Babel was built with stone slabs even though the term "brick" is used in Genesis 11:3. The historical reports state that it took a year to hoist material to the top of the Tower, which caused the people to cry when a brick fell. Surely the cry was not for a modern-day brick.

> The Tower had reached such a height that it took a whole year to hoist up necessary building-material to the top; in consequence, materials became so valuable that they cried when a brick fell and broke, while they remained indifferent when a man fell and was killed. (www.jewishencyclopedia.com)

The people who hoisted material to build the great tower would find it elementary to make and hoist stones to build a monument like Stonehenge. The people were skilled in brick (stone) making and not in stone transportation across the country. The materials to make the stones were easily transported across the country just as the materials to make the bricks at the Tower of Babel were brought in and hoisted up approximately a mile. If the materials were hoisted upward to the construction spots, that is the evidence that the stones were made on site as needed. The process involved mixing, pouring, drying, and sanding to a final finish. This process was used by the builders of Stonehenge and other megalithic sites as they labored to memorialize the work of the angels. The people were once again coordinating their collective strength to accomplish a great deed, but this time the deed was for honoring and thanking God.

The constructions of some of the standing stone monuments were not only memorials but also reactions to the eventual tapering off of the visitations after the crisis was alleviated. The healings by the angels did not end injury, disease, depression, and death. Mankind was still required to survive with the "thorns and thistles" of natural life.

Genesis 3:17–18: And unto Adam he said, "Because

thou hast hearkened unto the voice of thy wife, and hast eaten of the tree, of which I commanded thee, saying thou shalt not eat of it: cursed is the ground for thy sake; in sorrow shalt thou eat of it all the days of thy life; thorns also and thistles shall it bring forth to thee; and thou shalt eat the herb of the field."

The grandeur and significance of Stonehenge, which was built by the collective body of people, inspired individuals to mimic it on a much smaller scale. Archaeologists have discovered small ancient stone structures called "dolmen" whose patterns of construction are similar to Stonehenge. Dolmen are miniature Stonehenge in the fact that they are small standing stone pillars with a covering stone that brings to mind the lintel over the standing stones at Stonehenge.

**Figure 17. Dolmen**
**The famous Dolmen of Crucno, in the middle of a small Breton village. The chamber consists of nine pillars supporting a capstone weighing over 40 tons. (www. crystalinks.com/carnacstones.html)**

The dolmen monuments also represent the individual person's plea for healing of another person in the same manner as was accomplished at Stonehenge. But their pleas did not generate the same response as the natural catastrophes. Many sick and injured people were taken to the sites of the healings and to the dolmen, but there was never again any healing activities on such a grand scale. The pleas at the monuments were unanswered, and many who were taken to the sites grew worse and died. The monuments became historical places of healings whose status developed into local cemeteries. The people didn't understand that the mission of the angels was to improve the birth and death ratio for the propagation of mankind across the globe.

> Stonehenge was the biggest cemetery of its time, larger than fourteen other comparable cemeteries known elsewhere in Britain from the third millennium BC.
> (www.shef.ac.uk/archaeology/research/stonehenge/stonehenge07-01.html)

The idea of using stones as representations of experiences with God continued throughout history and is reflected in two biblical stories involving Jacob and stones. It seems that Jacob had a belief in stone displays as representations of experiences with God. He not only believed in creating the displays but also believed that God would honor them.

> Genesis 28:18, 22: And Jacob rose up early in the morning and took the stone that he had put for his pillows, and set it up for a pillar, and poured oil upon the top of it…. "And this stone, which I have set for a pillar, shall be God's house; and of all that thou shalt give me I will surely give the tenth unto thee."

> Genesis 35:13–15: And God went up from him in the place where he talked with him. And Jacob set up

a pillar in the place where he talked with him, even a pillar of stone; and he poured a drink offering on it, and he poured oil thereon. And Jacob called the name of the place where God spoke with him, Bethel.

The Scriptures show Jacob's way of signifying that something special had occurred in his relationship with God at a particular place. If he used a stone as a pillow for the night, the stone could not have been very large. Why were small stone pillars Jacob's choice, and why was he confident of their future significance? Is it possible that Jacob was inspired to erect stone pillars by his knowledge of the purpose of ancient stone monuments? I believe he knew that his pillars would be accepted by God and honored by the angels of God that visit the land, and they would supply the means whereby his plans would be fulfilled.

Men constructed Stonehenge and other megalithic monuments to commemorate the healing campaign of the angels. There are other constructions and patterns left by the angels that have their commemorative value as well, such as the following:

1. The perfect circles carved deep into the ground
2. The avenues lined with gypsum
3. Sillsbury Hill
4. The burnt mounds and their pools
5. The collections of human bones and animal parts

Archaeologists have noticed that many of the stone monuments and other excavated spaces seem to have arrangements that aligned with astrological points. If this is true, then those alignments are also memorials of the coming of angels. Angels would not use man-made tools of measurements, just as they didn't use man-made tools of construction. The angels are knowledgeable of the planetary alignments and points of axis and how the compass points register throughout the universe. Their measurements would be products of a grander calculation of geometric points applied to minute spaces on earth. Since man did not have advanced measuring tools, the angels used their knowledge to assist men in their constructions. That is why simple constructions of massive stones align with complex astrological measurements.

> There are indeed a large number of astronomical alignments, prediction and measuring devices, and representative features to be found among the megalithic stones and holes of Stonehenge. Gerald Hawkins discovered many of them, and most of his discoveries are commonly accepted.
> (www.tivas.org.uk/stonehenge/stone_ast.html)

> It is clear that the placement of stones in Stonehenge was planned. This could have been Stone Age brilliance, or it could have been just the moderately observant farmers' knowledge of the sky. Because we haven't found any written records from its makers, we just don't know!
> (www.windows2universe.org/the_universe/uts/stonehenge_astro.html)

# Conclusion

The scriptural realities that man was created tell us that the world of the Creator has knowledge of the composition, functionality, and frailties of mankind. The Creator, or God, has designated responsibilities to angels for the preservation of man, who is his most valued creation. Even though God once repented of making man, he has always come short of totally annihilating him. His love has always reserved a remnant for future propagation.

Commentaries by Bible scholars state there is a hierarchy of angels, which is indicative of an organized system of government. The biblical accounts of the interactions of angels with man show that the government of God is inclusive of man. Also, since the Bible indicates in the Book of Genesis that the conflict between God and the fallen angels had spread to the newly created Adam and Eve, then it was imperative that the power of heaven be applied to their preservation and development. Continuous assistance for survival and development was based on man's obedience to God. Man was denied the continuous luxury of the Garden of Eden due to his disobedience but was given a whole world in which to multiply and master. Man began to show a great propensity for disobedience, which developed into open defiance and caused God to respond in cataclysmic ways after periods of warnings. God imposed corrective actions that were far reaching geographically and along the timeline of man's existence.

Those actions include the Great Flood, the collapse of the Tower of Babel, the split of Pangaea, and the destruction of Sodom and Gomorrah. After each catastrophe, the intent was for man to reject his old ways and embark upon the new world with his efforts centered on the will of God.

Prior to the split of Pangaea, the issue that needed to be addressed in conjunction with disobedience was man's oneness: one leader, one language, one nation, one land, one general appearance, and one purpose for existence. The oneness caused men to focus on their own strength as their key to survival and gave them confidence to challenge the power of God. After the collapse of the Tower of Babel and the split of Pangaea, the people were forced into multiple leaders, multiple languages, multiple nations, the beginning of human physiological changes, multiple continents, and multiple purposes for existence as defined by each individual nation. The development of the multiplicities was in line with God's plan for mankind and the world.

During the ancient times of the megalithic era, man experienced the breakup of his physical world, which sent physical and emotional devastation throughout the population. Healing by the angels was the only solution to a worldwide crisis that had the potential of leading to the extinction of mankind. The angels arrived with one prime objective, which was to save mankind at all cost. The people of Shinar, who were striving to rival heaven through the strength of their number, found themselves needing unusual sacrifices of animals to survive. Man, who was made from the dust of the ground and akin to all flesh, was made to realize that, even though he was created a little lower than the angels, he was also created just a little higher than the animals. He began to realize that his uniqueness was the breath of life that God gave him.

Psalms 8:4–5: What is man, that thou art mindful of

him? And the son of man, that thou visitest him? For thou hast made him a little lower than the angels, and hast crowned him with glory and honor.

Genesis 2:7: And the Lord God formed man of the dust of the ground, and breathed into his nostrils the breath of life; and man became a living soul.

All men great or small were victims of the same catastrophe of the split of Pangaea. The victims of the split and the collapse of the Tower of Babel received a blessing of immense proportion, and it would be a tragedy not to mention their joy and gratitude for their preservation. I thought of their relief and praise as I read about the reactions of the Haitians after the earthquake of 2010 and the biblical account of the invalid at the Gate called Beautiful.

Everywhere we went, groups and churches were meeting to pray and give thanks to God for the safety of their surviving family members.... We rejoiced as we saw the Haitian people praising God and seeking him to heal their land.
(Washingtontimes.com, whatsupgundys.blogspot.com/2010/02/revival-in-haiti.html)

Acts 3:6–8: Then Peter said, "Silver and gold have I none, but, such as I have, give I thee. In the name of Jesus Christ of Nazareth, rise up and walk." And he took him by the right hand, and lifted him up; and immediately his feet and ankle bones received strength. And he, leaping up, stood and walked, and entered with them into the temple, walking, and leaping, and praising God.

The monuments are indeed spectacles that show great

gratitude to the work of the angels, but there is no greater display of gratitude than the praises that come from the mouths and souls of men. Yet, without the stones, who would realize that legions of angels descended from on high to initiate a massive healing campaign? The formations of the Carnac Stones and stone circles have prompted the people of modern times to ask, "What mean ye these stones?" Just as at the biblical event at the Jordan River, stones placed in a noticeable formation make the curious mind research their meaning. The displays had to be grand and sturdy enough to survive the ravages of time, nature, and man.

Men have been concerned about future catastrophes and the destruction of the planet, and they have calculated frequent timelines for destruction, which have resulted in failed predictions. They worry about the impending great earthquake, the possible collision of a killer asteroid, a nuclear Armageddon, and other catastrophes. But God has demonstrated his desire for man to continue upon this planet, and if it is his will, what can override it? While we wonder what dangers linger above and below us, we should understand that God has the answers and the resources to manage any catastrophe and to provide for the safety of the righteous. The Bible predicts many more catastrophes upon this earth, all of which will be punctuated by injury and death: earthquakes in diverse places, wars and rumors of wars, plagues, and so on. But men must recognize that disobedience to God has proven to be the greatest threat to their continuous existence. This fact is reflected in the Great Flood, the collapse of the Tower of Babel, the split of Pangaea, and the destruction of Sodom, Gomorrah, and the cities of the plain, and it will be reflected in the future prediction of the Battle at Armageddon, followed by the destruction of the heavens and earth.

The life of man and the fate of the world have always been and will always be in the hands of God, and the quality of his existence is relative to his relationship with God.

Angels have been assigned the tasks to provide warnings, defense, destruction, and healing for mankind based on this relationship. Healing has always been an integral part of God's plan for man, and healing has been performed on a grand scale for the masses and for individuals apart from the masses. At one point in ancient history, man lived with a vast company of angels who labored to heal him for his survival. The magnitude and duration of the healing event made it necessary for men to erect monuments to commemorate the angels' presence. They came and fulfilled their mission by gleaning from the resources available on earth. The recipients of their labor made their best effort to show the world that the angels were here in large numbers. The people erected stone monuments across the world that cannot be ignored and that produce questions as to their purposes. Modern man must discern the story in stone so that the efforts of the ancient people can receive their full recognition.

# Bibliography

Absolute Astronomy, www.absoluteastronomy.com/topics/
Aubrey_holes

A History of Glass Timeline, artantiques.allinfo-about.com/
features/glass_timeline

Answersingenesis.org, www.answersingenesis.org/creation/
v22/i1/peleg.asp

Archao News, www.stonepages.com/news/archives/000475.
html

Avebury, England, www.sacredsites.com/europe/england/
avebury.html

A-Z Animals, a-z-animals.com/animals/pig

BBC News, www.bbc.co.uk/history/programmes/
stonehenge/article1.shtml

BBC News, www.bbc.co.uk/history/programmes/
stonehenge/biographies.shtml

Biology-Online, www.biology-online.org/dictionary/Melanin

Christian Answers, www.christiananswers.net/q-aig/aig-c010.
html

CNN, www.cnn.com/2010/HEALTH/01/13/haiti.
earthquake.medical.risks/index.html

CNN, www.cnn.com/2005/TECH/02/23/spark.pigs/index.
html)

Counting Stones, www.philipcoppens.com/carnac.html

Crystalinks.com, www.crystalinks.com/avebury.html

Crystalinks.com, www.crystalinks.com/carnacstones.html

Crystalinks.com, www.crystalinks.com/gungywamp.html

Crystalinks.com, www.crystalinks.com/henge.html

Crystalinks.com, www.crystalinks.com/thornborough.html

Crystalinks.com, www.crystalinks.com/medicinewheel.html

Daily Bible Study, The Camp, www.keyway.ca/
htm2000/20001016.htm

Direct Industry, www.directindustry.com/prod/hunnebeck-
group-gmbh/circular-wall-formwork-57436-388705.html

ElectricScotland.com, www.electricscotland.com/stones/
loanhead.htm

Essentially England, www.essentially-england.com/
prehistoric-england.html

FAQS Abstracts, www.faqs.org/abstracts/Zoology-and-
wildlife-conservation/A-marriage-of-bone-and-nacre-
Clinical-experiments-aimed-at-reducing-bone-loss-in-
jaws-raise-a-raft-o.html

Fetal Pig Dissection Guide, www.goshen.edu/bio/PigBook/
humanpigcomparisonl)

Goseck Circle, Germany, www.stonepages.com/news/
archives/000475.html

The Herb Companion, www.herbcompanion.com/herb-
profiles/Velvet-antler.aspx

Heritage Key, heritage-key.com/britain/aubrey-holes

The Hob Goblin, thehobgoblin.blogspot.com/2009/10/
bluestonehenge.html

The *Independent*, www.independent.co.uk/life-style/health-
and-families/health-news/healing-powers-of-oysters-
could-mend-human-bones-395527.html

InternationalGeologicalCongress2008, www.cprm.gov.
br/33IGC/1342187.html

*Jewish Encyclopedia*, www.jewishencyclopedia.com

Maeshowe, Charles Tait. www.maeshowe.co.uk/maeshowe/
standing.html

Market Publishers, marketpublishers.com/lists/1481/news.
html

Medical News Today, www.medicalnewstoday.com/
articles/77365, Pig to Human Transplantation, Getting
Closer

Medicinenet.com, www.medterms.com/script/main/art.
asp?articlekey=4340

The MegalithicPortal, www.boston.com/travel/getaways/
africa/articles/2008/09/28/

The Modern Antiquarian, www.philipcoppens.com/carnac.
html

Mystery Hill, planetvermont.com/pvq/v9n1/megaliths.html

The National Institute of Health, www.nei.nih.gov/health/
anoph/anophthalmia.asp#a

*Nature*, www.nature.com/nature/journal/v120/n3011/
abs/120084d0.html

*Nature*, Xenotransplantation, www.nature.com

*The New Scofield Study Bible*

Olmos Dam, www.texasbeyondhistory.net/st-plains/images/
ap10.html

*Orlando Sentinel*, www.orlandosentinel.com/news/local/os-
doctors-back-from-haiti-20100119,0,3496454.story

The Pangaea Theory, library.thinkquest.org/17701/high/
pangaea/

Pearson Schools, www.pearsonschoolsandfecolleges.
co.uk/Secondary/History/14-/
OCRGCSESchoolsHistoryProject/Samples

The Restored Church of God, www.thercg.org/articles/
agms.html

Royal Alberta Museum, www.royalalbertamuseum.ca/
human/archaeo/Faq/_medwhls.htm

Rudling, David. "Chanctonbury Ring revisited, The
Excavation of 1988-91." UCL Field Archaeology Unit,
Institute of Archaeology, University College London,
31–34 Gordon Square, London, WC1 0PY.

Sacred Destinations, www.sacred-destinations.com/england/
   stonehenge

San Diego State Univ., www.geology.sdsu.edu/how_
   volcanoes_work/

ScienceDirect, Bone reactions to nacre injected
   percutaneously into the vertebrae of sheep, www.
   sciencedirect.com/science?_ob=ArticleURL&_
   udi=B6TWB-42397W16&_user=10&_
   coverDate=03%2F15%2F2001&_rdoc=1&_
   fmt=high&_orig=search&_sort=d&_
   docanchor=&view=c&_searchStrId=1225503202&_
   rerunOrigin=google&_acct=C000050221&_
   version=1&_urlVersion=0&_userid=10&md5=d9f26bf
   30928fd4f3096cd833906c89f)

Sillsbury Hill, witcombe.sbc.edu/earthmysteries/EMSilbury.
   html

Sillsbury Hill, www.essentially-england.com/prehistoric-
   england.html

Steyning, South Downs, www.steyningsouthdowns.com/
   places/chanctonbury_ring

Stonehenge, utopia.duth.gr/~eandriop/geom/stonehenge.
   pdf

ThroughtheSandGlass, throughthesandglass.typepad.com/
   through_the_sandglass/2009/10/liquefaction

Tijuanaco, Bolivia, www.world-mysteries.com/mpl_6.htm\

Trepanationguide.com, www.trepanationguide.com/

The University of Sheffield, www.shef.ac.uk/archaeology/
   staff/parker.html

US Geological Survey, pubs.usgs.gov/gip/dynamic/
   historical.html

Washingtontimes.com, whatsupgundys.blogspot.
   com/2010/02/revival-in-haiti.html

*Webster's Ninth New Collegiate Dictionary*

Wiki Answers.com wiki.answers.com/Q/Who_
   said_'Drastic_times_call_for_drastic_measures_and_

Wikipedia, en.wikipedia.org/wiki/Mass%E2%80%93energy_
   equivalence
Wikipedia, en.wikipedia.org/wiki/Nimrod
Wikipedia, en.wikipedia.org/wiki/Silbury_Hill
Wikipedia, en.wikipedia.org/wiki/Stonehenge#cite_note-7
Wikipedia, en.wikipedia.org/wiki/Tower_of_Babel
Wikipedia, en.wikipedia.org/wiki/United_Kingdom
Yahoo News, news.yahoo.com/s/ap/20100123/ap_on_re_
   la_am_ca/cb_haiti_